ORTHROS

ORTHROS
A Morning Service Handbook

PATERIKON PUBLICATIONS

2023

ORTHROS: *A Morning Service Handbook*

© 2023 PATERIKON PUBLICATIONS
ALL RIGHTS RESERVED

Scripture taken from the St. Athanasius Academy Septuagint™. Copyright © 2008 by St. Athanasius Academy of Orthodox Theology. Used by permission. All rights reserved.

ISBN: 9798396286399

PATERIKON
PUBLICATIONS

CONTENTS

INTRODUCTION	7
ORTHROS FOR SUNDAYS	9
ORTHROS FOR FEASTS	63
DAILY ORTHROS	107
LENTEN DAILY ORTHROS	149

PASCHA & RENEWAL WEEK

PANNYCHIS	201
RESURRECTION CEREMONY	211
ORTHROS FOR RESURRECTION	213
APPENDIX: PRIESTLY PRAYERS	231

INTRODUCTION

THE intent of this publication is to offer an English language service book for the various forms of Orthros (also known as Matins), to be used by the laity in accordance with common practice in the Greek Orthodox Archdiocese of America.

As the primary target of this publication is the layperson, we have chosen to offer unabbreviated service texts for each form of the Orthros, in order that one does not need to flip back and forth as might be found with other service texts intended for Reader and Chanter.

For clergy, we have added the 12 prayers recited during the SIX PSALMS as an Appendix to this volume.

PATERIKON PUBLICATIONS
June 4, 2023
Great and Holy Pentecost

THE SERVICE OF
ORTHROS
for Sunday Mornings

PRIEST:

BLESSED is our God always, now and forever and to the ages of ages. ℟. Amen.

Glory to You, our God, glory to You.

O HEAVENLY King, O Comforter, the Spirit of Truth, who are present everywhere and filling all things, the treasury of good things and giver of life: O come and abide in us, and cleanse us from every stain, and save our souls, O Good one.

The Trisagion & Lord's Prayer
READER:

Holy God, Holy Mighty, Holy Immortal, have mercy on us. (3)

Glory to the Father and to the Son and to the Holy Spirit. Both now and forever and to the ages of ages. Amen.

All-holy Trinity, have mercy on us, Lord, forgive our sins. Master, pardon our transgressions. Holy One, visit and heal our infirmities, for Your name's sake.

Lord, have mercy. (3)

Glory to the Father and to the Son and to the Holy Spirit. Both now and forever and to the ages of ages. Amen.

Our Father, who art in heaven, hallowed be Thy name. Thy kingdom come, Thy will be done on earth as it is in heaven. Give us this day our daily bread, and forgive us our trespasses as we forgive those who trespass against us. And lead us not into temptation, but deliver us from evil.

FOR SUNDAY MORNINGS 11

PRIEST:

For Thine is the kingdom and the power and the glory, of the Father and of the Son and of the Holy Spirit, now and forever and to the ages of ages. ℟. Amen.

The Troparia
READER:

SAVE, O Lord, Your people and bless Your inheritance. Grant victory to the faithful against the adversaries of the faith, and protect Your people by the power of Your Cross.

Glory to the Father and to the Son and to the Holy Spirit.

YOU who were raised upon the Cross with volition, grant to Your new community Your compassion, which bears its name in Your honor, O Christ our God; gladden now with all Your strength, O Lord, our faithful leaders believing, granting them all victories against opponents competing; may they have as an alliance with You, the weapon of peace, the trophy invincible.

Both now and forever and to the ages of ages. Amen.

O PROTECTION unashamed and most formidable, do not despise, O good one, any of our petitions, all-praised Lady Theotokos: Strengthen now the Orthodox community, save those whom you have elected to lead us, and supply them with victory from the heavenly heights; for you have given birth unto God, and you alone are blessed.

PRIEST:

HAVE mercy on us, O God, according to Your great mercy, we pray You, hear us and have mercy.

℟. Lord, have mercy. (3, after each petition)

Let us pray for pious and Orthodox Christians. ℟.

Again we pray for our Archbishop (name). ℟.

PRIEST:

For You are a merciful God who loves mankind, and to You we offer up glory, to the Father and to the Son and to the Holy Spirit, now and forever and to the ages of ages. ℟ Amen.

READER:

In the name of the Lord, Father give the blessing.

PRIEST:

GLORY to the holy and consubstantial, and life-giving, and undivided Trinity always, now and forever and to the ages of ages. ℟ Amen.

The Six Psalms
READER:

GLORY to God in the highest, and on earth peace, goodwill among men. (3)

O Lord, You shall open my lips, and my mouth will declare Your praise. (2)

Psalm 3

O Lord, why do those who afflict me multiply?

Many are those who rise up against me.

Many are those who say to my soul, "There is no salvation for him in his God."

But You, O Lord, are my protector, my glory and the One who lifts up my head.

I cried to the Lord with my voice, and He heard me from His holy hill.

I lay down and slept; I awoke, for the Lord will help me.

I will not be afraid of ten thousands of people who set themselves against me all around.

Arise, O Lord, and save me, O my God, for You struck all those who were foolishly at enmity with me; You broke the teeth of sinners.

Salvation is of the Lord, and Your blessing is upon Your people.

(and again)

I lay down and slept; I awoke, for the Lord will help me.

Psalm 37

O Lord, do not rebuke me in Your wrath, nor chasten me in Your anger.

For Your arrows are fixed in me, and Your hand rests on me.

There is no healing in my flesh because of Your wrath; there is no peace in my bones because of my sins.

For my transgressions rise up over my head; like a heavy burden they are heavy on me.

My wounds grow foul and fester because of my folly.

I suffer misery, and I am utterly bowed down; I go all the day long with a sad face.

For my loins are filled with mockeries, and there is no healing in my flesh.

I am afflicted and greatly humbled; I roar because of the groaning of my heart.

O Lord, all my desire is before You, and my groaning is not hidden from You.

My heart is troubled; my strength fails me, and the light of my eyes, even this is not with me.

My friends and neighbors draw near and stand against me, and my near of kin stand far off;

And those who seek my soul use violence, and those who seek evil for me speak folly; and they meditate on deceit all the day long.

But I like a deaf man do not hear, and I am like a mute who does not open his mouth.

I am like a man who does not hear, and who has no reproofs in his mouth.

For in You, O Lord, I hope; You will hear, O Lord my God.

For I said, "Let not my enemies rejoice over me, for when my foot was shaken, they boasted against me."

For I am ready for wounds, and my pain is continually with me.

For I will declare my transgression, and I will be anxious about my sin.

But my enemies live, and are become stronger than I; and those who hate me unjustly are multiplied;

Those who repaid me evil for good slandered me, because I pursue righteousness;

Do not forsake me, O Lord; O my God, do not depart from me;

Give heed to help me, O Lord of my salvation.

FOR SUNDAY MORNINGS

(and again)

Do not forsake me, O Lord; O my God, do not depart from me;

Give heed to help me, O Lord of my salvation.

Psalm 62

O GOD, my God, I rise early to be with You; my soul thirsts for You.

How often my flesh thirsts for You in a desolate, impassable, and waterless land.

So in the holy place I appear before You, to see Your power and Your glory.

Because Your mercy is better than life, my lips shall praise You.

Thus I will bless You in my life; I will lift up my hands in Your name.

May my soul be filled, as if with marrow and fatness, and my mouth shall sing praise to You with lips filled with rejoicing.

If I remembered You on my bed, I meditated on You at daybreak;

For You are my helper, and in the shelter of Your wings I will greatly rejoice.

My soul follows close behind You; Your right hand takes hold of me.

But they seek for my soul in vain; they shall go into the lowest parts of the earth. They shall be given over to the edge of the sword; they shall be a portion for foxes.

But the king shall be glad in God; all who swear by Him shall be praised, for the mouth that speaks unrighteous things is stopped.

(and again)

I meditated on You at daybreak; For You are my helper, and in the shelter of Your wings I will greatly rejoice.

My soul follows close behind You; Your right hand takes hold of me.

Glory to the Father and to the Son and to the Holy Spirit, both now and forever and to the ages of ages. Amen.

Alleluia, alleluia, alleluia; glory to You, O God. (3)

Lord, have mercy. (3)

Glory to the Father and to the Son and to the Holy Spirit, both now and forever and to the ages of ages. Amen.

Psalm 87

O LORD God of my salvation, I cry day and night before You.

Let my prayer come before You; incline Your ear to my supplication, O Lord.

For my soul is filled with sorrows, and my soul draws near to Hades;

I am counted among those who go down into the pit; I am like a helpless man, free among the dead;

Like slain men thrown down and sleeping in a grave, whom You remember no more, but they are removed from Your hand.

They laid me in the lowest pit, in dark places and in the shadow of death.

Your wrath rested upon me, and You brought all Your billows over me.

You removed my acquaintances far from me; they made me an abomination among themselves;

I was betrayed, and did not go forth. My eyes weakened from poverty;

O Lord, I cry to You the whole day long; I spread out my hands to You.

Will You work wonders for the dead? Or will physicians raise them up, and acknowledge You?

Shall anyone in the grave describe Your mercy and Your truth in destruction?

Shall Your wonders be known in darkness, and Your righteousness in a forgotten land?

But I cry to You, O Lord, and in the morning my prayer shall come near to You.

Why, O Lord, do You reject my soul, and turn away Your face from me?

I am poor and in troubles from my youth; but having been exalted, I was humbled and brought into despair.

Your fierce anger passed over me, and Your terrors greatly troubled me;

They compassed me like water all the day long; they surrounded me at once.

You removed far from me neighbor and friend, and my acquaintances because of my misery.

(and again)

O Lord God of my salvation, I cry day and night before You.

Let my prayer come before You; incline Your ear to my supplication, O Lord.

Psalm 102

BLESS the Lord, O my soul, and everything within me, bless His holy name.

Bless the Lord, O my soul, and forget not all His rewards:

Who is merciful to all your transgressions, who heals all your diseases,

Who redeems your life from corruption, who crowns you with mercy and compassion,

Who satisfies your desire with good things; and your youth is renewed like the eagle's.

The Lord shows mercies and judgment to all who are wronged.

He made known His ways to Moses, the things He willed to the sons of Israel.

The Lord is compassionate and merciful, slow to anger, and abounding in mercy. He will not become angry to the end, nor will He be wrathful forever;

He did not deal with us according to our sins, nor reward us according to our transgressions;

For according to the height of heaven from earth, so the Lord reigns in mercy over those who fear Him;

As far as the east is from the west, so He removes our transgressions from us.

As a father has compassion on his children, so the Lord has compassion on those who fear Him, for He knows how He formed us; He remembers we are dust.

As for man, his days are like grass, as a flower of the field, so he flourishes;

For the wind passes through it, and it shall not remain; and it shall no longer know its place.

But the mercy of the Lord is from age to age upon those who fear Him,

And His righteousness upon children's children, to such as keep His covenant and remember His commandments, to do them.

The Lord prepared His throne in heaven, and His Kingdom rules over all.

Bless the Lord, all you His angels, mighty in strength, who do His word, so as to hear the voice of His words.

Bless the Lord, all you His hosts, His ministers who do His will;

Bless the Lord, all His works, in all places of His dominion; Bless the Lord, O my soul.

(and again)

In all places of His dominion; Bless the Lord, O my soul.

Psalm 142

O LORD, hear my prayer; give ear to my supplication in Your truth; answer me in Your righteousness;

Do not enter into judgment with Your servant, for no one living shall become righteous in Your sight.

For the enemy persecuted my soul; he humbled my life to the ground;

He caused me to dwell in dark places as one long dead, and my spirit was in anguish within me; my heart was troubled within me.

I remembered the days of old, and I meditated on all Your works; I meditated on the works of Your hands.

I spread out my hands to You; my soul thirsts for You like a waterless land.

Hear me speedily, O Lord; my spirit faints within me;

Turn not Your face from me, lest I become like those who go down into the pit.

Cause me to hear Your mercy in the morning, for I hope in You;

Make me know, O Lord, the way wherein I should walk, for I lift up my soul to You.

Deliver me from my enemies, O Lord, for to You I flee for refuge. Teach me to do Your will, for You are my God;

Your good Spirit shall guide me in the land of uprightness. For Your name's sake, O Lord, give me life;

In Your righteousness You shall bring my soul out of affliction. In Your mercy You shall destroy my enemies;

You shall utterly destroy all who afflict my soul, for I am Your servant.

(and again)

Answer me, O Lord, in Your righteousness, and do not enter into judgment with Your servant. (2)

Your good Spirit shall guide me in the land of uprightness.

Glory to the Father and to the Son and to the Holy Spirit, both now and forever and to the ages of ages. Amen.

Alleluia, alleluia, alleluia; glory to You, O God. (3) Our hope, O Lord, glory to You.

The Litany of Peace
PRIEST:

In peace, let us pray to the Lord.
℟. Lord, have mercy. (after each petition)

For the peace from above and for the salvation of our souls, let us pray to the Lord. ℟.

For the peace of the whole world, for the stability of the holy churches of God, and for the unity of all, let us pray to the Lord. ℟.

For this holy house and for those who enter it with faith, reverence, and the fear of God, let us pray to the Lord. ℟.

For pious and Orthodox Christians, let us pray to the Lord. ℟.

For our Archbishop (name), for the honorable presbyterate, for the diaconate in Christ, and for all the clergy and the people, let us pray to the Lord. ℟.

For our country, for the president, and for all in public service, let us pray to the Lord. ℟.

For this city, and for every city and land, and for the faithful who live in them, let us pray to the Lord. ℟.

For favorable weather, for an abundance of the fruits of the earth, and for peaceful times, let us pray to the Lord. ℟.

For those who travel by land, sea, and air, for the sick, the suffering, the captives and for their salvation, let us pray to the Lord. ℟.

For our deliverance from all affliction, wrath, danger, and necessity, let us pray to the Lord. ℟.

Help us, save us, have mercy on us, and protect us, O God, by Your grace. ℟.

Commemorating our most holy, pure, blessed, and glorious Lady, the Theotokos and ever-virgin Mary, with all the saints, let us commend ourselves and one another and our whole life to Christ our God. ℟. To You, O Lord.

PRIEST:

For to You belong all glory, honor, and worship, to the Father and to the Son and to the Holy Spirit, now and forever and to the ages of ages. ℟. Amen.

The "God is the Lord"

The Choirs chant the GOD IS THE LORD in the mode of the Resurrectional Apolytikion as follows:

CHOIRS:

GOD is the Lord, and He revealed Himself to us. Blessed is he who comes in the name of the Lord. (Psalm 117:27, 26)

℣. Give thanks to the Lord, for He is good; for His mercy endures forever. (Psalm 117:1)

℟. God is the Lord...

℣. All the nations surrounded me, but in the name of the Lord I defended myself against them. (Psalm 117:10)

℟. God is the Lord...

℣. And this came about from the Lord, and it is wonderful in our eyes. (Psalm 117:23)

℟. God is the Lord...

The Apolytikia

Then the Choirs chant the APOLYTIKIA (Dismissal Hymns) according to the order prescribed in the Typikon.

Kathismata & Evlogitaria

According to the ancient order, after the APOLYTIKIA, the KATHISMATA divisions of the Psalter are read, that is the 2nd, 3rd, and 17th (the Amomos).

In the parishes, the Psalter reading is omitted, and straightway after the APOLYTIKIA, the Priest says the SMALL LITANY:

Again and again, in peace, let us pray to the Lord. ℟ Lord, have mercy. (after each)
Help us, save us, have mercy on us, and protect us, O God, by Your grace. ℟

Commemorating our most holy, pure, blessed, and glorious Lady, the Theotokos and ever-virgin Mary, with all the saints, let us commend ourselves and one another and our whole life to Christ our God. ℟ To You, O Lord.

PRIEST:

For Yours is the dominion, and Yours is the kingdom and the power and the glory, of the Father and of the Son and of the Holy Spirit, now and forever and to the ages of ages. ℟ Amen.

*The Choirs chant the Resurrectional Sessional Hymns (*KATHISMATA*) in succession, and straightway after these, they chant the* RESURRECTIONAL EVLOGITARIA.

*Resurrectional Evlogitaria
Plagal First Mode.*
CHOIRS:

℣. Blessed are You, O Lord, teach me Your commandments.

THE multitude of angels, was astonished to see You, accounted among the dead; Unto death, O Savior, You have destroyed all its might, and with Yourself You have also raised Adam, and from Hades have liberated everyone.

℣. Blessed are You, O Lord, teach me Your commandments.

WHY mingle the myrrh with tears of compassion, women disciples of the Lord? Thus the dazzling angel in the sepulcher addressed unto the myrrh-bearing women: Now you behold the empty tomb and understand, for the Savior has risen from the sepulcher.

℣. Blessed are You, O Lord, teach me Your commandments.

At early morn, the myrrh-bearers hastened, to Your sepulcher with lamentation; but standing by, was the Angel who said to the women: The time for lamenting has ceased, weep no longer; go tell the Apostles of the Resurrection.

℣. Blessed are You, O Lord, teach me Your commandments.

The myrrh-bearing women had arrived with their spices, unto Your tomb, O Savior, and they heard an Angel clearly announcing unto them: Why do you account the living among the dead? For, as God, He is risen from the sepulcher.

℣. Glory to the Father and to the Son and to the Holy Spirit.

Let us worship the Father, and He who is His very Son, also the Holy Spirit: the Holy Trinity, singular in its essence, with the Seraphim we now cry aloud: Holy, Holy, Holy are You, O Lord.

℣. Both now and forever and to the ages of ages. Amen.

By giving birth, O Virgin, unto the Giver of life, you redeemed Adam from sin, and you supplied unto Eve, joy in place of sorrow; He became from you, both God and Man incarnate, and directed back to life him who fell from it.

Alleluia, alleluia, alleluia; glory to You, O God. (3)

Straightway after the RESURRECTIONAL EVLOGITARIA, the Priest says the SMALL LITANY.

The Small Litany

Again and again, in peace, let us pray to the Lord. ℟. Lord, have mercy. (after each)

Help us, save us, have mercy on us, and protect us, O God, by Your grace. ℟.

Commemorating our most holy, pure, blessed, and glorious Lady, the Theotokos and ever-virgin Mary, with all the saints, let us commend ourselves and one another and our whole life to Christ our God. ℟. To You, O Lord.

PRIEST:

For blessed is Your name, and glorified is Your kingdom, of the Father and the Son and the Holy Spirit, now and forever and to the ages of ages. ℟. Amen.

Hypakoë - Anavathmoi - Prokeimenon

And the Reader recites the HYPAKOË of the mode.

The Choirs chant the ANAVATHMOI (Hymns of Ascent) and the PROKEIMENON of the mode.

If the CANONS will not be chanted, then the SMALL LITANY occurs immediately after the PROKEIMENON, followed by the RESURRECTIONAL KONTAKION and OIKOS, as found on page 34.

Otherwise the Choirs proceed with the CANONS as follows:

The Canons

For ordinary Sundays, the Resurrectional Canon of the mode and that of the saint of the day are chanted.

After the 3rd Ode, the Priest says the SMALL LITANY.

The Small Litany

Again and again, in peace, let us pray to the Lord. ℟. Lord, have mercy. (after each)

Help us, save us, have mercy on us, and protect us, O God, by Your grace. ℟.

Commemorating our most holy, pure, blessed, and glorious Lady, the Theotokos and ever-virgin Mary, with all the saints, let us commend ourselves and one another and our whole life to Christ our God. ℟. To You, O Lord.

PRIEST:

For You are our God, and to You we give glory, to the Father, the Son and the Holy Spirit, now and forever and to the ages of ages. ℟. Amen.

The Choirs chant the Mid-Ode Kathismata.

Immediately following the Mid-Ode Kathismata, or if the CANONS were not done, immediately following the PROKEIMENON, again the Priest says the SMALL LITANY.

The Small Litany

Again and again, in peace, let us pray to the Lord. ℟. Lord, have mercy. (after each)

Help us, save us, have mercy on us, and protect us, O God, by Your grace. ℟.

Commemorating our most holy, pure, blessed, and glorious Lady, the Theotokos and ever-virgin Mary, with all the saints, let us commend ourselves and one another and our whole life to Christ our God. ℟. To You, O Lord.

PRIEST:

For You are the King of peace and the Savior of our souls, and to You we offer up glory, to the Father and the Son and the Holy Spirit, now and forever and to the ages of ages. ℟. Amen.

Kontakion - Oikos - Synaxarion

And the Reader recites the KONTAKION, and OIKOS, as well as the SYNAXARION from the Menaion, except on the Sundays of the Triodion and Pentecostarion, as well as the Sunday of celebrated saints.

The Katavasias

After this, to complete the CANONS, the Choirs chant the KATAVASIAS of the period until the 8th Ode.

The KATAVASIA of the 8th Ode is preceded by the verse:

℣. We praise and we bless and we worship the Lord.

Following the KATAVASIA of the 8th Ode, the Deacon announces the EOTHINON (morning) Gospel reading.

The Eothinon Gospel

DEACON: Let us pray to the Lord. ℟. Lord, have mercy.

PRIEST:

For You are holy, our God, who rest among the saints, and to You we offer up glory, to the Father and the Son and the Holy Spirit, now and forever and to the ages of ages. ℟. Amen.

And the Choirs chant the fixed Prokeimenon as follows:

FIRST CHOIR: Let everything that breathes praise the Lord. (Psalm 150:6)

SECOND CHOIR: Let everything that breathes praise the Lord.

FIRST CHOIR:

℣. Praise God in His saints; praise Him in the firmament of His power. (Psalm 150:1)

Let everything that breathes…

SECOND CHOIR: Praise the Lord.

The Deacon says the following aloud from the Beautiful Gate:

DEACON: That we may be counted worthy to hear the Holy Gospel, let us entreat the Lord our God. ℟. Lord, have mercy. (3)

DEACON: Wisdom. Arise. Let us hear the Holy Gospel.

The Priest comes to the Beautiful Gate, blessing the people with his right hand, and says:

PRIEST: Peace be with all. ℟. And with your spirit.

PRIEST: The reading is from the Holy Gospel according to (name).

DEACON: Let us be attentive.

CHOIR: Glory to You, O Lord, glory to You.

The Priest reads the designated EOTHINON GOSPEL standing at the right of the holy Altar, with the Deacon standing opposite him.

CHOIR: Glory to You, O Lord, glory to You.

PROESTOS (OR READER):

Having seen the Resurrection of Christ, let us worship the holy Lord Jesus, the only sinless one. We venerate Your Cross, O Christ, and Your holy Resurrection we praise and glorify. For You are our God, and apart from You we know no other; we call upon Your name. Come, all the faithful, let us venerate the holy Resurrection of Christ. For behold, through the Cross, joy has come to the whole world. Ever blessing the Lord, we praise His Resurrection. For having endured the Cross for us, He destroyed death by death.

The 50th Psalm

The Choirs antiphonally chant the verses of the 50TH PSALM.

Have mercy on me, O God, according to Your great mercy; and according to the abundance of Your compassion, blot out my transgression.

Wash me thoroughly from my lawlessness and cleanse me from my sin.

For I know my lawlessness, and my sin is always before me.

Against You only have I sinned and done evil in Your sight; that You may be justified in Your words, and overcome when You are judged.

For behold, I was conceived in transgressions, and in sins my mother bore me.

Behold, You love truth; You showed me the unknown and secret things of Your wisdom.

You shall sprinkle me with hyssop, and I will be cleansed; You shall wash me, and I will be made whiter than snow.

You shall make me hear joy and gladness; my bones that were humbled shall greatly rejoice.

Turn Your face from my sins, and blot out all my transgressions.

FOR SUNDAY MORNINGS

Create in me a clean heart, O God, and renew a right spirit within me.

Do not cast me away from Your presence, and do not take Your Holy Spirit from me.

Restore to me the joy of Your salvation, and uphold me with Your guiding Spirit.

I will teach transgressors Your ways, and the ungodly shall turn back to You.

Deliver Me from bloodguiltiness, O God, the God of my salvation, and my tongue shall greatly rejoice in Your righteousness.

O Lord, You shall open my lips, and my mouth will declare Your praise.

For if You desired sacrifice, I would give it; You will not be pleased with whole burnt offerings.

A sacrifice to God is a broken spirit, a broken and humble heart God will not despise.

Do good, O Lord, in Your good pleasure to Zion, and let the walls of Jerusalem be built.

Then You will be pleased with a sacrifice of righteousness, with offerings and whole burnt offerings.

Then shall they offer young bulls on Your altar. And have mercy on me, O God.

After the psalm, the following Troparia are chanted in alternation in Second Mode:

FIRST CHOIR:

Glory to the Father and to the Son and to the Holy Spirit.

At the intercessions of the Apostles, O merciful One, blot out the multitude of my offenses.

SECOND CHOIR:

Both now and forever and to the ages of ages. Amen.

At the intercessions of the Theotokos, O merciful One, blot out the multitude of my offenses.

FIRST CHOIR:

℣. Have mercy on me, O God, according to Your great mercy; and according to the abundance of Your compassion, blot out my transgression. (Psalm 50:1)

And the Pentecostarion is chanted in the same mode.

FIRST CHOIR:

Jesus, having risen from the sepulcher, as He foretold, has given us eternal life, and great mercy.

According to the Sundays of the Triodion, instead of the above, chant what is below. Otherwise, proceed to intercession on page 42.

FIRST CHOIR:

Glory to the Father and to the Son and to the Holy Spirit.

Plagal Fourth Mode.

Open unto me the gates of repentance, O Life-giver; for early does my spirit rise towards Your most holy Temple, bearing my bodily temple wholly in defilement; but as compassionate, cleanse me, by Your tender-hearted mercy.

SECOND CHOIR:

Both now and forever and to the ages of ages. Amen.

Lead me on the paths of salvation, O Theotokos, for I have defiled my soul with shameful sins, having wasted my whole life in laziness; by your intercessions, deliver me from all impurity.

FIRST CHOIR:

℣. Have mercy on me, O God, according to Your great mercy; and according to the abundance of Your compassion, blot out my transgression. (Psalm 50:1)

Plagal Second Mode.
FIRST CHOIR:

When I, the wretched one, reflect upon the multitude of my terrible deeds, I tremble at that fearful day of judgment; but taking courage in the mercy of Your compassion, like David I cry unto You, "Have mercy on me, O God, according to Your great mercy."

After the Troparia, the Deacon or Priest says the following intercession:

O GOD, save Your people and bless Your inheritance; visit Your world with mercy and compassions; exalt the horn of the Orthodox Christians, and send down upon us Your abundant mercies; through the intercessions of our all-pure Lady the Theotokos and ever-virgin Mary; the power of the precious and life-giving Cross, the protection of the honorable, bodiless powers of heaven; the supplications of the honorable and glorious prophet and forerunner John the Baptist; of the holy, glorious, and praise-worthy apostles; our Fathers among the saints, the great hierarchs and ecumenical teachers, Basil the Great, Gregory the Theologian and John Chrysostom; Athanasios, Cyril, and John the Merciful, patriarchs of Alexandria; Nicholas, bishop of Myra, Spyridon, bishop of Trimythous, Nektarios of Pentapolis, the wonderworkers; the holy, glorious great martyrs George the Victorious, Demetrios the Myrobletes, Theodore the Teron, and Theodore the General, Menas the Wonderworker; the hieromartyrs Haralambos and Eleftherios; the holy, glorious, and victorious martyrs; the glorious great martyr and all-laudable Euphemia; the holy and glorious martyrs Thecla, Barbara, Anastasia, Katherine, Kyriake, Fotene, Marina, Paraskeve and Irene; of our holy God-bearing Fathers; (local patron saint); the holy and righteous ancestors of God Joachim and Anna; of (saint of the day) whose memory we celebrate; and of all Your saints. We beseech You, only merciful Lord, hear us sinners who pray to You and have mercy on us.

CHOIRS: Lord, have mercy. (12)

PRIEST:

Through the mercy, compassions, and benevolence of Your only-begotten Son, with whom You are blessed, together with Your all-holy, good and life-giving Spirit, now and forever and to the ages of ages. ℟. Amen.

The Ode of the Theotokos
DEACON:

Let us honor and magnify in song the Theotokos and the Mother of the light.

And the following verses of the ODE OF THE THEOTOKOS (Luke 1:46-55) are chanted by the Choirs.

℣. My soul magnifies the Lord, and my spirit has rejoiced in God my Savior.

MORE honorable than the Cherubim, and beyond compare more glorious than the Seraphim, without corruption you gave birth to God the Logos. We magnify you, the true Theotokos. (and so after each of the following verses.)

℣. For He has looked upon the humble state of His handmaid; for behold, from now on, all generations will call me blessed. ℟.

℣. For He who is mighty has done great things for me, and holy is His name, and His mercy is for generations of generations on those who fear Him. ℟.

℣. He has shown strength with His arm; He has scattered the proud in the imagination of their hearts. ℟.

℣. He has put down the mighty from their thrones, and exalted the humble. He has filled the hungry with good things, and He has sent the rich away empty. ℟.

℣. He has helped Israel His servant in remembrance of His mercy, as He spoke to our fathers, to Abraham and to his seed forever. ℟.

And the Choirs continue with chanting the 9th Ode of the CANON and its Katavasia.

Then the Priest or the Deacon says the SMALL LITANY.

The Small Litany

Again and again, in peace, let us pray to the Lord. ℟ Lord, have mercy. (after each)

Help us, save us, have mercy on us, and protect us, O God, by Your grace. ℟

Commemorating our most holy, pure, blessed, and glorious Lady, the Theotokos and ever-virgin Mary, with all the saints, let us commend ourselves and one another and our whole life to Christ our God. ℟ To You, O Lord.

PRIEST:

For all the powers of heaven praise You, and to You we offer up glory, to the Father, the Son and the Holy Spirit, now and forever and to the ages of ages. ℟ Amen.

The Exapostilaria

The Choirs alternately chant the following verses in the Second Mode.

FIRST CHOIR: Holy is the Lord our God.

SECOND CHOIR: Holy is the Lord our God.

FIRST CHOIR: Holy is the Lord our God. Exalt the Lord our God, and worship at the footstool of His feet.

SECOND CHOIR: For He is holy.

And the Resurrectional EXAPOSTILARION and its Theotokion are chanted. If there is also an EXAPOSTILARION in the Menaion, after the Resurrectional Exapostilarion, we omit its Theotokion, and chant that of the Menaion and its Theotokion.

The Praises

After the EXAPOSTILARIA, the PRAISES of the mode of Sunday, and the Resurrectional Stichera are chanted.

Psalm 148

LET everything that breathes praise the Lord. Praise the Lord from the heavens, praise Him in the highest. It is fitting to sing a hymn to You, O God.

PRAISE Him, all you His angels; praise Him, all you His hosts. It is fitting to sing a hymn to You, O God.[1]

Praise Him, sun and moon; praise Him, all you stars and light.

Praise Him, you heavens of heavens, and you waters above the heavens. Let them praise the Lord's name.

For He spoke, and they were made; He commanded, and they were created.

He established them forever and unto ages of ages; He set forth His ordinance, and it shall not pass away.

Praise the Lord from the earth, you dragons and all the deeps,

---

[1] If the intermediate verses are to be disregarded, then the first Choir advances to the verse *To fulfill among them the written judgment...*, from which the set of Stichera begins.

Fire and hail, snow and ice, stormy wind, which perform His word.

Mountains and all the hills, fruitful trees and all cedars,

Wild animals and all cattle, creeping things and flying birds,

Kings of the earth and all peoples, princes and all judges of the earth.

Young men and maidens, elders with younger; let them praise the Lord's name, for His name alone is exalted.

His thanksgiving is in earth and heaven. And He shall exalt the horn of His people.

A hymn for all His saints, for the children of Israel, a people who draw near to Him.

Psalm 149

Sing to the Lord a new song, His praise in the assembly of His holy ones.

Let Israel be glad in Him who made him, and let the children of Zion greatly rejoice in their King.

Let them praise His name with dance; with tambourine and harp let them sing to Him;

For the Lord is pleased with His people, and He shall exalt the gentle with salvation.

The holy ones shall boast in glory, and they shall greatly rejoice on their beds.

The high praise of God shall be in their mouth and a two-edged sword in their hand.

To deal retribution to the nations, reproving among the peoples.

To shackle their kings with chains and their nobles with fetters of iron.

The Stichera are attached to the following:

To fulfill among them the written judgment: this glory have all His holy ones.

Psalm 150

Praise God in His saints; praise Him in the firmament of His power.

Praise Him for His mighty acts; praise Him according to the abundance of His greatness.

Praise Him with the sound of a trumpet; praise Him with the harp and lyre;

Praise Him with timbrel and dance; praise Him with strings and flute;

Praise Him with resounding cymbals; praise Him with triumphant cymbals; Let everything that breathes praise the Lord.

The following two verses are added:

℣. Arise, O Lord my God, let Your hand be lifted high, and do not forget Your poor to the end. (Psalm 9:33)

℣. I will give thanks to You, O Lord, with my whole heart; I will tell of all Your wondrous things. (Psalm 9:1)

If, however, it is a Sunday of a coinciding feast which has its own set of verses, chant those prescribed for the feast.

FIRST CHOIR:
Glory to the Father and to the Son and to the Holy Spirit.

And they chant the prescribed Eothinon. *On the Sundays of the Triodion and Pentecostarion, chant the* Doxastikon *of Sunday. On the Sundays of feasts, chant the prescribed* Doxastikon *of the feast.*

SECOND CHOIR:

Both now and forever and to the ages of ages. Amen.

And they chant the present Theotokion:

You are most-blessed, O Virgin Theotokos; for through Him who was incarnate from you, Hades was made captive, Adam was recalled, the curse has been annulled, and Eve has been liberated; death has been put to death, and we have been brought to life. Therefore with hymns we cry aloud: Blessed are You, O Christ our God, who has been thus well pleased, glory to You.

And straightway the GREAT DOXOLOGY is chanted:

The Great Doxology

Glory to You who showed forth the light. Glory to God in the highest, and on earth peace, goodwill among men.

We praise You, we bless You, we worship You, we glorify You, we give thanks to You for Your great glory.

FOR SUNDAY MORNINGS

O Lord, King, O heavenly God, the Father Almighty, O Lord the only-begotten Son, O Jesus Christ, and the Holy Spirit.

O Lord, God, Lamb of God, Son of the Father, who take away the sin of the world: have mercy on us, You who take away the sins of the world.

Receive our prayer, You who sit at the right hand of the Father, and have mercy on us.

For You alone are holy; You alone are Lord, Jesus Christ, to the glory of God the Father. Amen.

Every day I will bless You, and I will praise Your name forever and unto the ages of ages.

Vouchsafe, O Lord, that on this day we be kept without sin.

Blessed are You, O Lord, God of our fathers, and praised and glorified is Your name unto the ages. Amen.

O Lord, let Your mercy be upon us for we have set our hope in You.

Blessed are You, O Lord, teach me Your commandments. (3)

O Lord, You have been our refuge from generation to generation. I said: O Lord, have mercy on me; heal my soul, for I have sinned against You.

O Lord, to You have I fled for refuge; teach me to do Your will, for You are my God.

For in You is the fountain of life; in Your light we shall see light.

Continue Your mercy unto those who know You.

Holy God, Holy Mighty, Holy Immortal, have mercy on us. (3)

Glory to the Father and to the Son and to the Holy Spirit;

Both now and forever and to the ages of ages. Amen.

Holy Immortal, have mercy on us.

Holy God, Holy Mighty, Holy Immortal, have mercy on us.

The Resurrectional Troparion

The Choir chants the RESURRECTIONAL TROPARION.

Fourth Mode.

TODAY salvation has come to the world. Let us sing to Him who arose from the tomb and is the Author of our life; for, destroying death by death, He granted us the victory and the great mercy.

FOR SUNDAY MORNINGS

In the parishes, while the GREAT DOXOLOGY *is chanted, the* SUPPLICATIONS, COMPLETION LITANY, PRAYER AT THE BOWING OF THE HEADS, *and the* DISMISSAL *of Orthros are said quietly by the Deacon and Priest.*

The Divine Liturgy begins immediately following the RESURRECTIONAL TROPARION.

The Supplications
DEACON:

HAVE mercy on us, O God, according to Your great mercy, we pray You, hear us and have mercy.

℟. Lord, have mercy. (3)

Again we pray for pious and Orthodox Christians. ℟.

Again we pray for our Archbishop (name). ℟.

Again we pray for our brethren: the priests, the hieromonks, the deacons, the monastics, and all our brotherhood in Christ. ℟.

Again we pray for mercy, life, peace, health, salvation, protection, forgiveness, and remission of the sins of the servants of

God, all pious Orthodox Christians residing and visiting the city: the parishioners, the members of the parish council, the stewards, and benefactors of this holy church. ℟.

Again we pray for the blessed and ever-memorable founders of this holy church, and for all our fathers and brethren who have fallen asleep before us, who here have been piously laid to their rest, as well as the Orthodox everywhere. ℟.

Again we pray for those who bear fruit and do good works in this holy and all-venerable church, for those who labor and those who sing, and for the people here present who await Your great and rich mercy. ℟.

PRIEST:

For You are a merciful God and love mankind, and to You we offer up glory, to the Father and to the Son and to the Holy Spirit, now and forever and to the ages of ages. ℟. Amen.

The Litany of Completion
DEACON:

LET us complete our morning prayer to the Lord.

℟. Lord, have mercy. (for first two petitions)

Help us, save us, have mercy on us, and protect us, O God, by Your grace. ℟.

That the whole day may be perfect, holy, peaceful, and sinless, let us ask the Lord.
℟. Grant this, O Lord. (after each petition)

For an angel of peace, a faithful guide, a guardian of our souls and bodies, let us ask the Lord. ℟.

For pardon and remission of our sins and transgressions, let us ask the Lord. ℟.

For that which is good and beneficial for our souls, and for peace for the world, let us ask the Lord. ℟.

That we may complete the remaining time of our life in peace and repentance, let us ask the Lord. ℟.

And let us ask for a Christian end to our life, peaceful, without shame and suffering, and for a good defense before the awesome judgment seat of Christ. ℟.

Commemorating our most holy, pure, blessed, and glorious Lady, the Theotokos and ever-virgin Mary, with all the saints, let us commend ourselves and one another and our whole life to Christ our God. ℟. To You, O Lord.

PRIEST:

For You are a God of mercy and compassion who loves mankind, and to You we give glory, to the Father and to the Son and to the Holy Spirit, now and forever and to the ages of ages. ℟. Amen.

And the Priest turns to face the people in order to offer them a blessing of peace.

Peace be with all. ℟. And with your spirit.

DEACON: Let us bow our heads to the Lord. ℟. To You, O Lord.

The Prayer at the Bowing of the Heads
PRIEST:

O HOLY Lord, who dwell on high and watch over the lowly, and who with Your all-seeing eye look upon all creation, to You have we bowed the neck of our soul and body, and we entreat You, O Holy of Holies: Stretch forth Your invisible hand from Your holy dwelling place and bless us all; and if in any way we have sinned, whether voluntarily or involuntarily, pardon us, as You are a good God and love mankind, granting us Your good things in this world and in the world to come.

Then the Priest exclaims:

For Yours it is to show mercy and to save us, O our God, and to You we offer up glory, to the Father and to the Son and to the Holy Spirit, now and forever and to ages of ages. ℟ Amen.

Following the PRAYER AT THE BOWING OF THE HEADS, the Deacon proclaims: Wisdom. ℟ Give the blessing.

PRIEST:

Blessed is He who is, Christ our God, always, now and forever and to the ages of ages. ℟ Amen.

DEACON:

May the Lord God strengthen the holy and pure faith of devout and Orthodox Christians, together with His holy Church, and this city, unto the ages of ages. ℟ Amen.

PRIEST:

Glory to You, Christ God, our hope, glory to You.

DEACON:

Glory to the Father and to the Son and to the Holy Spirit. Both now and forever and to the ages of ages. Amen. Lord, have mercy (3). Holy Father, give the blessing.

The Great Dismissal

Now the Priest does the GREAT DISMISSAL, saying: May He who rose from the dead... or on Feasts of the Master, its characteristic phrase.

MAY Christ our true God, through the intercessions of His all-pure and all-immaculate holy Mother; the power of the precious and life-giving Cross; the protection of the honorable, bodiless powers of heaven; the supplications of the honorable, glorious prophet and forerunner John the Baptist; of the holy, glorious, and praiseworthy apostles; of the holy, glorious, and triumphant martyrs; of our righteous and God-bearing Fathers; of (the saint of the church); of the holy and righteous ancestors of God Joachim and Anna; of (the saint of the day), whose memory we celebrate; and of all the saints; have mercy on us and save us, for He is good and loves mankind.

Through the prayers of our holy fathers, Lord Jesus Christ, our God, have mercy on us. ℟ Amen.

THE SERVICE OF
FESTAL ORTHROS
for feasts of the Master, Theotokos & Saints

PRIEST:

BLESSED is our God always, now and forever and to the ages of ages. ℟. Amen.

Glory to You, our God, glory to You.

O HEAVENLY King, O Comforter, the Spirit of Truth, who are present everywhere and filling all things, the treasury of good things and giver of life: O come and abide in us, and cleanse us from every stain, and save our souls, O Good one.

The Trisagion & Lord's Prayer
READER:

Holy God, Holy Mighty, Holy Immortal, have mercy on us. (3)

Glory to the Father and to the Son and to the Holy Spirit. Both now and forever and to the ages of ages. Amen.

All-holy Trinity, have mercy on us, Lord, forgive our sins. Master, pardon our transgressions. Holy One, visit and heal our infirmities, for Your name's sake.

Lord, have mercy. (3)

Glory to the Father and to the Son and to the Holy Spirit. Both now and forever and to the ages of ages. Amen.

Our Father, who art in heaven, hallowed be Thy name. Thy kingdom come, Thy will be done on earth as it is in heaven. Give us this day our daily bread, and forgive us our trespasses as we forgive those who trespass against us. And lead us not into temptation, but deliver us from evil.

PRIEST:

For Thine is the kingdom and the power and the glory, of the Father and of the Son and of the Holy Spirit, now and forever and to the ages of ages. ℟. Amen.

The Troparia
READER:

Save, O Lord, Your people and bless Your inheritance. Grant victory to the faithful against the adversaries of the faith, and protect Your people by the power of Your Cross.

Glory to the Father and to the Son and to the Holy Spirit.

You who were raised upon the Cross with volition, grant to Your new community Your compassion, which bears its name in Your honor, O Christ our God; gladden now with all Your strength, O Lord, our faithful leaders believing, granting them all victories against opponents competing; may they have as an alliance with You, the weapon of peace, the trophy invincible.

Both now and forever and to the ages of ages. Amen.

O PROTECTION unashamed and most formidable, do not despise, O good one, any of our petitions, all-praised Lady Theotokos: Strengthen now the Orthodox community, save those whom you have elected to lead us, and supply them with victory from the heavenly heights; for you have given birth unto God, and you alone are blessed.

PRIEST:

HAVE mercy on us, O God, according to Your great mercy, we pray You, hear us and have mercy.

℟. Lord, have mercy. (3, after each petition)

Let us pray for pious and Orthodox Christians. ℟.

Again we pray for our Archbishop (name). ℟.

PRIEST:

For You are a merciful God who loves mankind, and to You we offer up glory, to the Father and to the Son and to the Holy Spirit, now and forever and to the ages of ages. ℟ Amen.

READER:

In the name of the Lord, Father give the blessing.

PRIEST:

Glory to the holy and consubstantial, and life-giving, and undivided Trinity always, now and forever and to the ages of ages. ℟ Amen.

The Six Psalms

READER:

Glory to God in the highest, and on earth peace, goodwill among men. (3)

O Lord, You shall open my lips, and my mouth will declare Your praise. (2)

Psalm 3

O Lord, why do those who afflict me multiply?

Many are those who rise up against me.

Many are those who say to my soul, "There is no salvation for him in his God."

But You, O Lord, are my protector, my glory and the One who lifts up my head.

I cried to the Lord with my voice, and He heard me from His holy hill.

I lay down and slept; I awoke, for the Lord will help me.

I will not be afraid of ten thousands of people who set themselves against me all around.

Arise, O Lord, and save me, O my God, for You struck all those who were foolishly at enmity with me; You broke the teeth of sinners.

Salvation is of the Lord, and Your blessing is upon Your people.

(and again)

I lay down and slept; I awoke, for the Lord will help me.

Psalm 37

O LORD, do not rebuke me in Your wrath, nor chasten me in Your anger.

For Your arrows are fixed in me, and Your hand rests on me.

There is no healing in my flesh because of Your wrath; there is no peace in my bones because of my sins.

For my transgressions rise up over my head; like a heavy burden they are heavy on me.

My wounds grow foul and fester because of my folly.

I suffer misery, and I am utterly bowed down; I go all the day long with a sad face.

For my loins are filled with mockeries, and there is no healing in my flesh.

I am afflicted and greatly humbled; I roar because of the groaning of my heart.

O Lord, all my desire is before You, and my groaning is not hidden from You.

My heart is troubled; my strength fails me, and the light of my eyes, even this is not with me.

My friends and neighbors draw near and stand against me, and my near of kin stand far off;

And those who seek my soul use violence, and those who seek evil for me speak folly; and they meditate on deceit all the day long.

But I like a deaf man do not hear, and I am like a mute who does not open his mouth.

I am like a man who does not hear, and who has no reproofs in his mouth.

For in You, O Lord, I hope; You will hear, O Lord my God.

For I said, "Let not my enemies rejoice over me, for when my foot was shaken, they boasted against me."

For I am ready for wounds, and my pain is continually with me.

For I will declare my transgression, and I will be anxious about my sin.

But my enemies live, and are become stronger than I; and those who hate me unjustly are multiplied;

Those who repaid me evil for good slandered me, because I pursue righteousness;

Do not forsake me, O Lord; O my God, do not depart from me;

Give heed to help me, O Lord of my salvation.

(and again)

Do not forsake me, O Lord; O my God, do not depart from me;

Give heed to help me, O Lord of my salvation.

Psalm 62

O GOD, my God, I rise early to be with You; my soul thirsts for You.

How often my flesh thirsts for You in a desolate, impassable, and waterless land.

So in the holy place I appear before You, to see Your power and Your glory.

Because Your mercy is better than life, my lips shall praise You.

Thus I will bless You in my life; I will lift up my hands in Your name.

May my soul be filled, as if with marrow and fatness, and my mouth shall sing praise to You with lips filled with rejoicing.

If I remembered You on my bed, I meditated on You at daybreak;

For You are my helper, and in the shelter of Your wings I will greatly rejoice.

My soul follows close behind You; Your right hand takes hold of me.

But they seek for my soul in vain; they shall go into the lowest parts of the earth. They shall be given over to the edge of the sword; they shall be a portion for foxes.

But the king shall be glad in God; all who swear by Him shall be praised, for the mouth that speaks unrighteous things is stopped.

(and again)

I meditated on You at daybreak; For You are my helper, and in the shelter of Your wings I will greatly rejoice.

My soul follows close behind You; Your right hand takes hold of me.

Glory to the Father and to the Son and to the Holy Spirit, both now and forever and to the ages of ages. Amen.

Alleluia, alleluia, alleluia; glory to You, O God. (3)

Lord, have mercy. (3)

Glory to the Father and to the Son and to the Holy Spirit, both now and forever and to the ages of ages. Amen.

Psalm 87

O LORD God of my salvation, I cry day and night before You.

Let my prayer come before You; incline Your ear to my supplication, O Lord.

For my soul is filled with sorrows, and my soul draws near to Hades;

I am counted among those who go down into the pit; I am like a helpless man, free among the dead;

Like slain men thrown down and sleeping in a grave, whom You remember no more, but they are removed from Your hand.

They laid me in the lowest pit, in dark places and in the shadow of death.

Your wrath rested upon me, and You brought all Your billows over me.

You removed my acquaintances far from me; they made me an abomination among themselves;

I was betrayed, and did not go forth. My eyes weakened from poverty;

O Lord, I cry to You the whole day long; I spread out my hands to You.

Will You work wonders for the dead? Or will physicians raise them up, and acknowledge You?

Shall anyone in the grave describe Your mercy and Your truth in destruction?

Shall Your wonders be known in darkness, and Your righteousness in a forgotten land?

But I cry to You, O Lord, and in the morning my prayer shall come near to You.

Why, O Lord, do You reject my soul, and turn away Your face from me?

I am poor and in troubles from my youth; but having been exalted, I was humbled and brought into despair.

Your fierce anger passed over me, and Your terrors greatly troubled me;

They compassed me like water all the day long; they surrounded me at once.

You removed far from me neighbor and friend, and my acquaintances because of my misery.

(and again)

O Lord God of my salvation, I cry day and night before You.

Let my prayer come before You; incline Your ear to my supplication, O Lord.

Psalm 102

BLESS the Lord, O my soul, and everything within me, bless His holy name.

Bless the Lord, O my soul, and forget not all His rewards:

Who is merciful to all your transgressions, who heals all your diseases,

Who redeems your life from corruption, who crowns you with mercy and compassion,

Who satisfies your desire with good things; and your youth is renewed like the eagle's.

The Lord shows mercies and judgment to all who are wronged.

He made known His ways to Moses, the things He willed to the sons of Israel.

The Lord is compassionate and merciful, slow to anger, and abounding in mercy. He will not become angry to the end, nor will He be wrathful forever;

He did not deal with us according to our sins, nor reward us according to our transgressions;

For according to the height of heaven from earth, so the Lord reigns in mercy over those who fear Him;

As far as the east is from the west, so He removes our transgressions from us.

As a father has compassion on his children, so the Lord has compassion on those who fear Him, for He knows how He formed us; He remembers we are dust.

As for man, his days are like grass, as a flower of the field, so he flourishes;

For the wind passes through it, and it shall not remain; and it shall no longer know its place.

But the mercy of the Lord is from age to age upon those who fear Him,

And His righteousness upon children's children, to such as keep His covenant and remember His commandments, to do them.

The Lord prepared His throne in heaven, and His Kingdom rules over all.

Bless the Lord, all you His angels, mighty in strength, who do His word, so as to hear the voice of His words.

Bless the Lord, all you His hosts, His ministers who do His will;

Bless the Lord, all His works, in all places of His dominion; Bless the Lord, O my soul.

(and again)

In all places of His dominion; Bless the Lord, O my soul.

Psalm 142

O Lord, hear my prayer; give ear to my supplication in Your truth; answer me in Your righteousness;

Do not enter into judgment with Your servant, for no one living shall become righteous in Your sight.

For the enemy persecuted my soul; he humbled my life to the ground;

He caused me to dwell in dark places as one long dead, and my spirit was in anguish within me; my heart was troubled within me.

I remembered the days of old, and I meditated on all Your works; I meditated on the works of Your hands.

I spread out my hands to You; my soul thirsts for You like a waterless land.

Hear me speedily, O Lord; my spirit faints within me;

Turn not Your face from me, lest I become like those who go down into the pit.

Cause me to hear Your mercy in the morning, for I hope in You;

Make me know, O Lord, the way wherein I should walk, for I lift up my soul to You.

Deliver me from my enemies, O Lord, for to You I flee for refuge. Teach me to do Your will, for You are my God;

Your good Spirit shall guide me in the land of uprightness. For Your name's sake, O Lord, give me life;

In Your righteousness You shall bring my soul out of affliction. In Your mercy You shall destroy my enemies;

You shall utterly destroy all who afflict my soul, for I am Your servant.

(and again)

Answer me, O Lord, in Your righteousness, and do not enter into judgment with Your servant. (2)

Your good Spirit shall guide me in the land of uprightness.

Glory to the Father and to the Son and to the Holy Spirit, both now and forever and to the ages of ages. Amen.

Alleluia, alleluia, alleluia; glory to You, O God. (3) Our hope, O Lord, glory to You.

The Litany of Peace
PRIEST:

In peace, let us pray to the Lord.
℟. Lord, have mercy. (after each petition)

For the peace from above and for the salvation of our souls, let us pray to the Lord. ℟.

For the peace of the whole world, for the stability of the holy churches of God, and for the unity of all, let us pray to the Lord. ℟.

For this holy house and for those who enter it with faith, reverence, and the fear of God, let us pray to the Lord. ℟.

For pious and Orthodox Christians, let us pray to the Lord. ℟.

For our Archbishop (name), for the honorable presbyterate, for the diaconate in Christ, and for all the clergy and the people, let us pray to the Lord. ℟.

For our country, for the president, and for all in public service, let us pray to the Lord. ℟.

For this city, and for every city and land, and for the faithful who live in them, let us pray to the Lord. ℟.

For favorable weather, for an abundance of the fruits of the earth, and for peaceful times, let us pray to the Lord. ℟.

For those who travel by land, sea, and air, for the sick, the suffering, the captives and for their salvation, let us pray to the Lord. ℟.

For our deliverance from all affliction, wrath, danger, and necessity, let us pray to the Lord. ℟.

Help us, save us, have mercy on us, and protect us, O God, by Your grace. ℟.

Commemorating our most holy, pure, blessed, and glorious Lady, the Theotokos and ever-virgin Mary, with all the saints, let us commend ourselves and one another and our whole life to Christ our God. ℟. To You, O Lord.

PRIEST:

For to You belong all glory, honor, and worship, to the Father and to the Son and to the Holy Spirit, now and forever and to the ages of ages. ℟. Amen.

The "God is the Lord"

The Choirs chant the GOD IS THE LORD in the mode of the Apolytikion as follows:

CHOIRS:

God is the Lord, and He revealed Himself to us. Blessed is he who comes in the name of the Lord. (Psalm 117:27, 26)

℣. Give thanks to the Lord, for He is good; for His mercy endures forever. (Psalm 117:1)

℟. God is the Lord…

℣. All the nations surrounded me, but in the name of the Lord I defended myself against them. (Psalm 117:10)

℟. God is the Lord…

℣. And this came about from the Lord, and it is wonderful in our eyes. (Psalm 117:23)

℟. God is the Lord…

The Apolytikion & Theotokion

Then the Choirs chant the APOLYTIKION (Dismissal Hymn) according to the order prescribed in the Typikon, along with its corresponding THEOTOKION in the same mode.

Kathismata

According to the ancient order, after the APOLYTIKIA, the KATHISMATA divisions of the Psalter are read, and the Polyeleos.

In the parishes, the Psalter reading is omitted, and straightway after the APOLYTIKIA, the Priest says the SMALL LITANY:

The Small Litany

Again and again, in peace, let us pray to the Lord. ℟. Lord, have mercy. (after each)

Help us, save us, have mercy on us, and protect us, O God, by Your grace. ℟.

Commemorating our most holy, pure, blessed, and glorious Lady, the Theotokos and ever-virgin Mary, with all the saints, let us commend ourselves and one another and our whole life to Christ our God. ℟. To You, O Lord.

PRIEST:

For Yours is the dominion, and Yours is the kingdom and the power and the glory, of the Father and of the Son and of the Holy Spirit, now and forever and to the ages of ages. ℟. Amen.

*The Choirs chant the Sessional Hymns (*KATHISMATA*) according to their order in the Menaion, then straightway they chant the first antiphon of the* ANAVATHMOI *(Hymns of Ascent) and the Prokeimenon of the feast.*

The First Antiphon of the Anavathmoi Fourth Mode.

From the time of my youth, plenty passions persecute me; but You who are my Savior, now help me and save me. (2)

You haters of Zion shall be put to shame by the Lord; for like the grass, by the fire you shall all be withered. (2)

Glory to the Father and to the Son and to the Holy Spirit.

By the Holy Spirit, every soul is made living, is exalted and shining by the cleansing of the Triple Unity in a hidden and sacred way.

Both now and forever and to the ages of ages. Amen.

By the Holy Spirit, the streams of grace are flowing, watering all of the creation unto the begetting of life.

And the Prokeimenon of the feast is chanted.

The Gospel

DEACON: Let us pray to the Lord. ℟. Lord, have mercy.

PRIEST:

For You are holy, our God, who rest among the saints, and to You we offer up glory, to the Father and the Son and the Holy Spirit, now and forever and to the ages of ages. ℟. Amen.

And the Choirs chant the fixed Prokeimenon as follows:

FIRST CHOIR: Let everything that breathes praise the Lord. (Psalm 150:6)

SECOND CHOIR: Let everything that breathes praise the Lord.

FIRST CHOIR:

℣. Praise God in His saints; praise Him in the firmament of His power. (Psalm 150:1)

Let everything that breathes...

SECOND CHOIR: Praise the Lord.

FOR FEASTS

The Deacon says the following aloud from the Beautiful Gate:

DEACON: That we may be counted worthy to hear the Holy Gospel, let us entreat the Lord our God. ℟ Lord, have mercy. (3)

DEACON: Wisdom. Arise. Let us hear the Holy Gospel.

The Priest comes to the Beautiful Gate, blessing the people with his right hand, and says:

PRIEST: Peace be with all. ℟ And with your spirit.

PRIEST: The reading is from the Holy Gospel according to (name).

DEACON: Let us be attentive.

CHOIR: Glory to You, O Lord, glory to You.

The Priest reads the designated GOSPEL *of the feast from the Beautiful Gate.*

CHOIR: Glory to You, O Lord, glory to You.

The 50th Psalm
PROESTOS (OR READER):

HAVE mercy on me, O God, according to Your great mercy; and according to the abundance of Your compassion, blot out my transgression.

Wash me thoroughly from my lawlessness and cleanse me from my sin.

For I know my lawlessness, and my sin is always before me.

Against You only have I sinned and done evil in Your sight; that You may be justified in Your words, and overcome when You are judged.

For behold, I was conceived in transgressions, and in sins my mother bore me.

Behold, You love truth; You showed me the unknown and secret things of Your wisdom.

You shall sprinkle me with hyssop, and I will be cleansed; You shall wash me, and I will be made whiter than snow.

You shall make me hear joy and gladness; my bones that were humbled shall greatly rejoice.

Turn Your face from my sins, and blot out all my transgressions.

Create in me a clean heart, O God, and renew a right spirit within me.

Do not cast me away from Your presence, and do not take Your Holy Spirit from me.

Restore to me the joy of Your salvation, and uphold me with Your guiding Spirit.

I will teach transgressors Your ways, and the ungodly shall turn back to You.

Deliver Me from bloodguiltiness, O God, the God of my salvation, and my tongue shall greatly rejoice in Your righteousness.

O Lord, You shall open my lips, and my mouth will declare Your praise.

For if You desired sacrifice, I would give it; You will not be pleased with whole burnt offerings.

A sacrifice to God is a broken spirit, a broken and humble heart God will not despise.

Do good, O Lord, in Your good pleasure to Zion, and let the walls of Jerusalem be built.

Then You will be pleased with a sacrifice of righteousness, with offerings and whole burnt offerings.

Then shall they offer young bulls on Your altar.

Following the reading of the 50TH PSALM, the Choirs chant the corresponding Troparia.

After the Troparia, the Deacon or Priest says the following intercession:

O GOD, save Your people and bless Your inheritance; visit Your world with mercy and compassions; exalt the horn of the Orthodox Christians, and send down upon us Your abundant mercies; through the intercessions of our all-pure Lady the Theotokos and ever-virgin Mary; the power of the precious and life-giving Cross, the protection of the honorable, bodiless powers of heaven; the supplications of the honorable and glorious prophet and forerunner John the Baptist; of the holy, glorious, and praiseworthy apostles; our Fathers among the saints, the great hierarchs and ecumenical teachers, Basil the Great, Gregory the Theologian and John Chrysostom; Athanasios, Cyril, and John the Merciful, patriarchs of Alexandria; Nicholas, bishop of Myra, Spyridon, bishop of Trimythous, Nektarios of Pentapolis, the wonderworkers; the holy, glorious great martyrs George the Victorious, Demetrios the Myrobletes, Theodore the Teron, and Theodore the General, Menas the Wonderworker; the hieromartyrs Haralambos and Eleftherios; the holy, glorious, and victorious martyrs; the glorious great martyr and all-laudable Euphemia; the holy and glorious martyrs Thecla, Barbara, Anastasia, Katherine, Kyriake, Fotene, Marina, Paraskeve and Irene; of our holy God-bearing Fathers; (local patron saint); the holy and righteous ancestors of God Joachim and Anna; of (saint of the day) whose memory we celebrate; and of all Your saints. We beseech You, only merciful Lord, hear us sinners who pray to You and have mercy on us. ℞ Lord, have mercy. (12)

PRIEST:

Through the mercy, compassions, and benevolence of Your only-begotten Son, with whom You are blessed, together with Your all-holy, good and life-giving Spirit, now and forever and to the ages of ages. ℞ Amen.

If the CANONS will not be chanted, then straightway read the KONTAKION, OIKOS, and SYNAXARION, continued on page 92.

※※※※※

Otherwise the Choirs proceed as follows:
The Canons
After the 3rd Ode, the Priest says the SMALL LITANY.

The Small Litany
Again and again, in peace, let us pray to the Lord. ℟. Lord, have mercy. (after each)

Help us, save us, have mercy on us, and protect us, O God, by Your grace. ℟.

Commemorating our most holy, pure, blessed, and glorious Lady, the Theotokos and ever-virgin Mary, with all the saints, let us commend ourselves and one another and our whole life to Christ our God. ℟. To You, O Lord.

PRIEST:
For You are our God, and to You we give glory, to the Father, the Son and the Holy Spirit, now and forever and to the ages of ages. ℟. Amen.

The Choirs chant the Mid-Ode Kathismata, or recite the HYPAKOË in its place if one is designated.

Immediately following the Mid-Ode Kathismata, again the Priest says the SMALL LITANY.

The Small Litany
Again and again, in peace, let us pray to the Lord. ℟ Lord, have mercy. (after each)

Help us, save us, have mercy on us, and protect us, O God, by Your grace. ℟

Commemorating our most holy, pure, blessed, and glorious Lady, the Theotokos and ever-virgin Mary, with all the saints, let us commend ourselves and one another and our whole life to Christ our God. ℟ To You, O Lord.

PRIEST:
For You are the King of peace and the Savior of our souls, and to You we offer up glory, to the Father and the Son and the Holy Spirit, now and forever and to the ages of ages. ℟ Amen.

Kontakion - Oikos - Synaxarion

And the Reader recites the KONTAKION, and OIKOS, as well as the SYNAXARION.

The Katavasias

After this, to complete the CANONS, the Choirs chant the KATAVASIAS of the feast until the 8th Ode.

The KATAVASIA of the 8th Ode is preceded by the verse:

℣. We praise and we bless and we worship the Lord.

Following the KATAVASIA of the 8th Ode, the Deacon announces the ODE OF THE THEOTOKOS and proceeds to cense the entire church.

The Ode of the Theotokos
DEACON:

Let us honor and magnify in song the Theotokos and the Mother of the light.

And the Choirs chant either the "More honorable..." or the Megalynaria of the 9th Ode with verses, as prescribed, and the KATAVASIA.

Then the Priest or the Deacon says the SMALL LITANY.

The Small Litany

Again and again, in peace, let us pray to the Lord. ℟ Lord, have mercy. (after each)

Help us, save us, have mercy on us, and protect us, O God, by Your grace. ℟

Commemorating our most holy, pure, blessed, and glorious Lady, the Theotokos and ever-virgin Mary, with all the saints, let us commend ourselves and one another and our whole life to Christ our God. ℟ To You, O Lord.

PRIEST:

For all the powers of heaven praise You, and to You we offer up glory, to the Father, the Son and the Holy Spirit, now and forever and to the ages of ages. ℟ Amen.

The Exapostilarion

The Choirs chant the designated EXAPOSTILARION with its corresponding Theotokion. For great feasts, it may be chanted thrice with no prescribed Theotokion.

The Praises

After the EXAPOSTILARION, the PRAISES are chanted along with the designated Stichera for the feast.

Psalm 148

LET everything that breathes praise the Lord. Praise the Lord from the heavens, praise Him in the highest. It is fitting to sing a hymn to You, O God.

PRAISE Him, all you His angels; praise Him, all you His hosts. It is fitting to sing a hymn to You, O God.

Praise Him, sun and moon; praise Him, all you stars and light.

Praise Him, you heavens of heavens, and you waters above the heavens. Let them praise the Lord's name.

For He spoke, and they were made; He commanded, and they were created.

He established them forever and unto ages of ages; He set forth His ordinance, and it shall not pass away.

Praise the Lord from the earth, you dragons and all the deeps,

Fire and hail, snow and ice, stormy wind, which perform His word.

Mountains and all the hills, fruitful trees and all cedars,

Wild animals and all cattle, creeping things and flying birds,

Kings of the earth and all peoples, princes and all judges of the earth.

Young men and maidens, elders with younger; let them praise the Lord's name, for His name alone is exalted.

His thanksgiving is in earth and heaven. And He shall exalt the horn of His people.

A hymn for all His saints, for the children of Israel, a people who draw near to Him.

Psalm 149

Sing to the Lord a new song, His praise in the assembly of His holy ones.

Let Israel be glad in Him who made him, and let the children of Zion greatly rejoice in their King.

Let them praise His name with dance; with tambourine and harp let them sing to Him;

For the Lord is pleased with His people, and He shall exalt the gentle with salvation.

The holy ones shall boast in glory, and they shall greatly rejoice on their beds.

The high praise of God shall be in their mouth and a two-edged sword in their hand.

To deal retribution to the nations, reproving among the peoples.

To shackle their kings with chains and their nobles with fetters of iron.

To fulfill among them the written judgment: this glory have all His holy ones.

Psalm 150

Praise God in His saints; praise Him in the firmament of His power.

Praise Him for His mighty acts; praise Him according to the abundance of His greatness.

Praise Him with the sound of a trumpet; praise Him with the harp and lyre;

Praise Him with timbrel and dance; praise Him with strings and flute;

Praise Him with resounding cymbals; praise Him with triumphant cymbals; Let everything that breathes praise the Lord.

FIRST CHOIR:

Glory to the Father and to the Son and to the Holy Spirit.

And they chant the prescribed Doxastikon.

SECOND CHOIR:

Both now and forever and to the ages of ages. Amen.

And they chant the prescribed Theotokion.

And straightway the GREAT DOXOLOGY is chanted:

The Great Doxology

GLORY to You who showed forth the light. Glory to God in the highest, and on earth peace, goodwill among men.

We praise You, we bless You, we worship You, we glorify You, we give thanks to You for Your great glory.

O Lord, King, O heavenly God, the Father Almighty, O Lord the only-begotten Son, O Jesus Christ, and the Holy Spirit.

O Lord, God, Lamb of God, Son of the Father, who take away the sin of the world: have mercy on us, You who take away the sins of the world.

Receive our prayer, You who sit at the right hand of the Father, and have mercy on us.

For You alone are holy; You alone are Lord, Jesus Christ, to the glory of God the Father. Amen.

Every day I will bless You, and I will praise Your name forever and unto the ages of ages.

Vouchsafe, O Lord, that on this day we be kept without sin.

FOR FEASTS

Blessed are You, O Lord, God of our fathers, and praised and glorified is Your name unto the ages. Amen.

O Lord, let Your mercy be upon us for we have set our hope in You.

Blessed are You, O Lord, teach me Your commandments. (3)

O Lord, You have been our refuge from generation to generation. I said: O Lord, have mercy on me; heal my soul, for I have sinned against You.

O Lord, to You have I fled for refuge; teach me to do Your will, for You are my God.

For in You is the fountain of life; in Your light we shall see light.

Continue Your mercy unto those who know You.

Holy God, Holy Mighty, Holy Immortal, have mercy on us. (3)

Glory to the Father and to the Son and to the Holy Spirit;

Both now and forever and to the ages of ages. Amen.

Holy Immortal, have mercy on us.

Holy God, Holy Mighty, Holy Immortal, have mercy on us.

The Apolytikion

Then the Choir chants the APOLYTIKION of the feast or the saint.

In the parishes, while the GREAT DOXOLOGY is chanted, the SUPPLICATIONS, COMPLETION LITANY, PRAYER AT THE BOWING OF THE HEADS, and the DISMISSAL of Orthros are said quietly by the Deacon and Priest.

The Divine Liturgy begins immediately following the APOLYTIKION.

The Supplications
DEACON:

HAVE mercy on us, O God, according to Your great mercy, we pray You, hear us and have mercy.

℟. Lord, have mercy. (3)

Again we pray for pious and Orthodox Christians. ℟.

Again we pray for our Archbishop (name). ℟.

Again we pray for our brethren: the priests, the hieromonks, the deacons, the monastics, and all our brotherhood in Christ. ℟.

Again we pray for mercy, life, peace, health, salvation, protection, forgiveness, and remission of the sins of the servants of God, all pious Orthodox Christians residing and visiting the city: the parishioners, the members of the parish council, the stewards, and benefactors of this holy church. ℟.

Again we pray for the blessed and ever-memorable founders of this holy church, and for all our fathers and brethren who have fallen asleep before us, who here have been piously laid to their rest, as well as the Orthodox everywhere. ℟.

Again we pray for those who bear fruit and do good works in this holy and all-venerable church, for those who labor and those who sing, and for the people here present who await Your great and rich mercy. ℟.

PRIEST:

For You are a merciful God and love mankind, and to You we offer up glory, to the Father and to the Son and to the Holy Spirit, now and forever and to the ages of ages. ℟. Amen.

The Litany of Completion
DEACON:

Let us complete our morning prayer to the Lord.

℞. Lord, have mercy. (for first two petitions)

Help us, save us, have mercy on us, and protect us, O God, by Your grace. ℞.

That the whole day may be perfect, holy, peaceful, and sinless, let us ask the Lord.

℞. Grant this, O Lord. (after each petition)

For an angel of peace, a faithful guide, a guardian of our souls and bodies, let us ask the Lord. ℞.

For pardon and remission of our sins and transgressions, let us ask the Lord. ℞.

For that which is good and beneficial for our souls, and for peace for the world, let us ask the Lord. ℞.

That we may complete the remaining time of our life in peace and repentance, let us ask the Lord. ℞.

And let us ask for a Christian end to our life, peaceful, without shame and suffering, and for a good defense before the awesome judgment seat of Christ. ℟.

Commemorating our most holy, pure, blessed, and glorious Lady, the Theotokos and ever-virgin Mary, with all the saints, let us commend ourselves and one another and our whole life to Christ our God. ℟. To You, O Lord.

PRIEST:

For You are a God of mercy and compassion who loves mankind, and to You we give glory, to the Father and to the Son and to the Holy Spirit, now and forever and to the ages of ages. ℟. Amen.

And the Priest turns to face the people in order to offer them a blessing of peace.

Peace be with all. ℟. And with your spirit.

DEACON: Let us bow our heads to the Lord. ℟. To You, O Lord.

The Prayer at the Bowing of the Heads
PRIEST:

O HOLY Lord, who dwell on high and watch over the lowly, and who with Your all-seeing eye look upon all creation, to You have we bowed the neck of our soul and body, and we entreat You, O Holy of Holies: Stretch forth Your invisible hand from Your holy dwelling place and bless us all; and if in any way we have sinned, whether voluntarily or involuntarily, pardon us, as You are a good God and love mankind, granting us Your good things in this world and in the world to come.

Then the Priest exclaims:

For Yours it is to show mercy and to save us, O our God, and to You we offer up glory, to the Father and to the Son and to the Holy Spirit, now and forever and to ages of ages. ℟ Amen.

Following the PRAYER AT THE BOWING OF THE HEADS, the Deacon proclaims: Wisdom. ℟ Give the blessing.

PRIEST:

Blessed is He who is, Christ our God, always, now and forever and to the ages of ages. ℟. Amen.

DEACON:

May the Lord God strengthen the holy and pure faith of devout and Orthodox Christians, together with His holy Church, and this city, unto the ages of ages. ℟. Amen.

PRIEST:

Glory to You, Christ God, our hope, glory to You.

DEACON:

Glory to the Father and to the Son and to the Holy Spirit. Both now and forever and to the ages of ages. Amen. Lord, have mercy (3). Holy Father, give the blessing.

The Great Dismissal

Now the Priest does the GREAT DISMISSAL. If it is a feast of the Master, begin with its characteristic phrase. Otherwise as follows:

May Christ our true God, through the intercessions of His all-pure and all-immaculate holy Mother; the power of the precious and life-giving Cross; the protection of the honorable, bodiless powers of heaven; the supplications of the honorable, glorious prophet and forerunner John the Baptist; of the holy, glorious, and praiseworthy apostles; of the holy, glorious, and triumphant martyrs; of our righteous and God-bearing Fathers; of (the saint of the church); of the holy and righteous ancestors of God Joachim and Anna; of (the saint of the day), whose memory we celebrate; and of all the saints; have mercy on us and save us, for He is good and loves mankind.

Through the prayers of our holy fathers, Lord Jesus Christ, our God, have mercy on us. ℟. Amen.

THE SERVICE OF
DAILY ORTHROS
from Monday to Friday,
& Saturdays with "God is the Lord"

PRIEST:

BLESSED is our God always, now and forever and to the ages of ages. ℟ Amen.

Glory to You, our God, glory to You.

O HEAVENLY King, O Comforter, the Spirit of Truth, who are present everywhere and filling all things, the treasury of good things and giver of life: O come and abide in us, and cleanse us from every stain, and save our souls, O Good one.

The Trisagion & Lord's Prayer

READER:

Holy God, Holy Mighty, Holy Immortal, have mercy on us. (3)

Glory to the Father and to the Son and to the Holy Spirit. Both now and forever and to the ages of ages. Amen.

All-holy Trinity, have mercy on us, Lord, forgive our sins. Master, pardon our transgressions. Holy One, visit and heal our infirmities, for Your name's sake.

Lord, have mercy. (3)

Glory to the Father and to the Son and to the Holy Spirit. Both now and forever and to the ages of ages. Amen.

Our Father, who art in heaven, hallowed be Thy name. Thy kingdom come, Thy will be done on earth as it is in heaven. Give us this day our daily bread, and forgive us our trespasses as we forgive those who trespass against us. And lead us not into temptation, but deliver us from evil.

PRIEST:

For Thine is the kingdom and the power and the glory, of the Father and of the Son and of the Holy Spirit, now and forever and to the ages of ages. ℟ Amen.

The Troparia
READER:

Save, O Lord, Your people and bless Your inheritance. Grant victory to the faithful against the adversaries of the faith, and protect Your people by the power of Your Cross.

Glory to the Father and to the Son and to the Holy Spirit.

You who were raised upon the Cross with volition, grant to Your new community Your compassion, which bears its name in Your honor, O Christ our God; gladden now with all Your strength, O Lord, our faithful leaders believing, granting them all victories against opponents competing; may they have as an alliance with You, the weapon of peace, the trophy invincible.

Both now and forever and to the ages of ages. Amen.

O PROTECTION unashamed and most formidable, do not despise, O good one, any of our petitions, all-praised Lady Theotokos: Strengthen now the Orthodox community, save those whom you have elected to lead us, and supply them with victory from the heavenly heights; for you have given birth unto God, and you alone are blessed.

PRIEST:

HAVE mercy on us, O God, according to Your great mercy, we pray You, hear us and have mercy.

℟. Lord, have mercy. (3, after each petition)

Let us pray for pious and Orthodox Christians. ℟.

Again we pray for our Archbishop (name). ℟.

PRIEST:

For You are a merciful God who loves mankind, and to You we offer up glory, to the Father and to the Son and to the Holy Spirit, now and forever and to the ages of ages. ℞ Amen.

READER:

In the name of the Lord, Father give the blessing.

PRIEST:

Glory to the holy and consubstantial, and life-giving, and undivided Trinity always, now and forever and to the ages of ages. ℞ Amen.

The Six Psalms
READER:

Glory to God in the highest, and on earth peace, goodwill among men. (3)

O Lord, You shall open my lips, and my mouth will declare Your praise. (2)

Psalm 3

O Lord, why do those who afflict me multiply?

Many are those who rise up against me.

Many are those who say to my soul, "There is no salvation for him in his God."

But You, O Lord, are my protector, my glory and the One who lifts up my head.

I cried to the Lord with my voice, and He heard me from His holy hill.

I lay down and slept; I awoke, for the Lord will help me.

I will not be afraid of ten thousands of people who set themselves against me all around.

Arise, O Lord, and save me, O my God, for You struck all those who were foolishly at enmity with me; You broke the teeth of sinners.

Salvation is of the Lord, and Your blessing is upon Your people.

(and again)

I lay down and slept; I awoke, for the Lord will help me.

Psalm 37

O Lord, do not rebuke me in Your wrath, nor chasten me in Your anger.

For Your arrows are fixed in me, and Your hand rests on me.

There is no healing in my flesh because of Your wrath; there is no peace in my bones because of my sins.

For my transgressions rise up over my head; like a heavy burden they are heavy on me.

My wounds grow foul and fester because of my folly.

I suffer misery, and I am utterly bowed down; I go all the day long with a sad face.

For my loins are filled with mockeries, and there is no healing in my flesh.

I am afflicted and greatly humbled; I roar because of the groaning of my heart.

O Lord, all my desire is before You, and my groaning is not hidden from You.

My heart is troubled; my strength fails me, and the light of my eyes, even this is not with me.

My friends and neighbors draw near and stand against me, and my near of kin stand far off;

And those who seek my soul use violence, and those who seek evil for me speak folly; and they meditate on deceit all the day long.

But I like a deaf man do not hear, and I am like a mute who does not open his mouth.

I am like a man who does not hear, and who has no reproofs in his mouth.

For in You, O Lord, I hope; You will hear, O Lord my God.

For I said, "Let not my enemies rejoice over me, for when my foot was shaken, they boasted against me."

For I am ready for wounds, and my pain is continually with me.

For I will declare my transgression, and I will be anxious about my sin.

But my enemies live, and are become stronger than I; and those who hate me unjustly are multiplied;

Those who repaid me evil for good slandered me, because I pursue righteousness;

Do not forsake me, O Lord; O my God, do not depart from me;

Give heed to help me, O Lord of my salvation.

(and again)

Do not forsake me, O Lord; O my God, do not depart from me;

Give heed to help me, O Lord of my salvation.

Psalm 62

O GOD, my God, I rise early to be with You; my soul thirsts for You.

How often my flesh thirsts for You in a desolate, impassable, and waterless land.

So in the holy place I appear before You, to see Your power and Your glory.

Because Your mercy is better than life, my lips shall praise You.

Thus I will bless You in my life; I will lift up my hands in Your name.

May my soul be filled, as if with marrow and fatness, and my mouth shall sing praise to You with lips filled with rejoicing.

If I remembered You on my bed, I meditated on You at daybreak;

For You are my helper, and in the shelter of Your wings I will greatly rejoice.

My soul follows close behind You; Your right hand takes hold of me.

But they seek for my soul in vain; they shall go into the lowest parts of the earth. They shall be given over to the edge of the sword; they shall be a portion for foxes.

But the king shall be glad in God; all who swear by Him shall be praised, for the mouth that speaks unrighteous things is stopped.

(and again)

I meditated on You at daybreak; For You are my helper, and in the shelter of Your wings I will greatly rejoice.

My soul follows close behind You; Your right hand takes hold of me.

Glory to the Father and to the Son and to the Holy Spirit, both now and forever and to the ages of ages. Amen.

Alleluia, alleluia, alleluia; glory to You, O God. (3)

Lord, have mercy. (3)

Glory to the Father and to the Son and to the Holy Spirit, both now and forever and to the ages of ages. Amen.

Psalm 87

O Lord God of my salvation, I cry day and night before You.

Let my prayer come before You; incline Your ear to my supplication, O Lord.

For my soul is filled with sorrows, and my soul draws near to Hades;

I am counted among those who go down into the pit; I am like a helpless man, free among the dead;

Like slain men thrown down and sleeping in a grave, whom You remember no more, but they are removed from Your hand.

They laid me in the lowest pit, in dark places and in the shadow of death.

Your wrath rested upon me, and You brought all Your billows over me.

You removed my acquaintances far from me; they made me an abomination among themselves;

I was betrayed, and did not go forth. My eyes weakened from poverty;

O Lord, I cry to You the whole day long; I spread out my hands to You.

Will You work wonders for the dead? Or will physicians raise them up, and acknowledge You?

Shall anyone in the grave describe Your mercy and Your truth in destruction?

Shall Your wonders be known in darkness, and Your righteousness in a forgotten land?

But I cry to You, O Lord, and in the morning my prayer shall come near to You.

Why, O Lord, do You reject my soul, and turn away Your face from me?

I am poor and in troubles from my youth; but having been exalted, I was humbled and brought into despair.

Your fierce anger passed over me, and Your terrors greatly troubled me;

They compassed me like water all the day long; they surrounded me at once.

You removed far from me neighbor and friend, and my acquaintances because of my misery.

(and again)

O Lord God of my salvation, I cry day and night before You.

Let my prayer come before You; incline Your ear to my supplication, O Lord.

Psalm 102

BLESS the Lord, O my soul, and everything within me, bless His holy name.

Bless the Lord, O my soul, and forget not all His rewards:

Who is merciful to all your transgressions, who heals all your diseases,

Who redeems your life from corruption, who crowns you with mercy and compassion,

Who satisfies your desire with good things; and your youth is renewed like the eagle's.

The Lord shows mercies and judgment to all who are wronged.

He made known His ways to Moses, the things He willed to the sons of Israel.

The Lord is compassionate and merciful, slow to anger, and abounding in mercy. He will not become angry to the end, nor will He be wrathful forever;

He did not deal with us according to our sins, nor reward us according to our transgressions;

For according to the height of heaven from earth, so the Lord reigns in mercy over those who fear Him;

As far as the east is from the west, so He removes our transgressions from us.

As a father has compassion on his children, so the Lord has compassion on those who fear Him, for He knows how He formed us; He remembers we are dust.

As for man, his days are like grass, as a flower of the field, so he flourishes;

For the wind passes through it, and it shall not remain; and it shall no longer know its place.

But the mercy of the Lord is from age to age upon those who fear Him,

And His righteousness upon children's children, to such as keep His covenant and remember His commandments, to do them.

The Lord prepared His throne in heaven, and His Kingdom rules over all.

Bless the Lord, all you His angels, mighty in strength, who do His word, so as to hear the voice of His words.

Bless the Lord, all you His hosts, His ministers who do His will;

Bless the Lord, all His works, in all places of His dominion; Bless the Lord, O my soul.

(and again)

In all places of His dominion; Bless the Lord, O my soul.

Psalm 142

O Lord, hear my prayer; give ear to my supplication in Your truth; answer me in Your righteousness;

Do not enter into judgment with Your servant, for no one living shall become righteous in Your sight.

For the enemy persecuted my soul; he humbled my life to the ground;

He caused me to dwell in dark places as one long dead, and my spirit was in anguish within me; my heart was troubled within me.

I remembered the days of old, and I meditated on all Your works; I meditated on the works of Your hands.

I spread out my hands to You; my soul thirsts for You like a waterless land.

Hear me speedily, O Lord; my spirit faints within me;

Turn not Your face from me, lest I become like those who go down into the pit.

Cause me to hear Your mercy in the morning, for I hope in You;

Make me know, O Lord, the way wherein I should walk, for I lift up my soul to You.

Deliver me from my enemies, O Lord, for to You I flee for refuge. Teach me to do Your will, for You are my God;

Your good Spirit shall guide me in the land of uprightness. For Your name's sake, O Lord, give me life;

In Your righteousness You shall bring my soul out of affliction. In Your mercy You shall destroy my enemies;

You shall utterly destroy all who afflict my soul, for I am Your servant.

(and again)

Answer me, O Lord, in Your righteousness, and do not enter into judgment with Your servant. (2)

Your good Spirit shall guide me in the land of uprightness.

Glory to the Father and to the Son and to the Holy Spirit, both now and forever and to the ages of ages. Amen.

Alleluia, alleluia, alleluia; glory to You, O God. (3) Our hope, O Lord, glory to You.

The Litany of Peace
PRIEST:

IN peace, let us pray to the Lord.
℟. Lord, have mercy. (after each petition)

For the peace from above and for the salvation of our souls, let us pray to the Lord. ℟.

For the peace of the whole world, for the stability of the holy churches of God, and for the unity of all, let us pray to the Lord. ℟.

For this holy house and for those who enter it with faith, reverence, and the fear of God, let us pray to the Lord. ℟.

For pious and Orthodox Christians, let us pray to the Lord. ℟.

For our Archbishop (name), for the honorable presbyterate, for the diaconate in Christ, and for all the clergy and the people, let us pray to the Lord. ℟.

For our country, for the president, and for all in public service, let us pray to the Lord. ℟.

For this city, and for every city and land, and for the faithful who live in them, let us pray to the Lord. ℟.

For favorable weather, for an abundance of the fruits of the earth, and for peaceful times, let us pray to the Lord. ℟.

For those who travel by land, sea, and air, for the sick, the suffering, the captives and for their salvation, let us pray to the Lord. ℟.

For our deliverance from all affliction, wrath, danger, and necessity, let us pray to the Lord. ℟.

Help us, save us, have mercy on us, and protect us, O God, by Your grace. ℟.

Commemorating our most holy, pure, blessed, and glorious Lady, the Theotokos and ever-virgin Mary, with all the saints, let us commend ourselves and one another and our whole life to Christ our God. ℟. To You, O Lord.

PRIEST:

For to You belong all glory, honor, and worship, to the Father and to the Son and to the Holy Spirit, now and forever and to the ages of ages. ℟. Amen.

The "God is the Lord"

The Choirs chant the GOD IS THE LORD in the mode of the Apolytikion as follows:

CHOIRS:

GOD is the Lord, and He revealed Himself to us. Blessed is he who comes in the name of the Lord. (Psalm 117:27, 26)

℣. Give thanks to the Lord, for He is good; for His mercy endures forever. (Psalm 117:1)

℟. God is the Lord...

℣. All the nations surrounded me, but in the name of the Lord I defended myself against them. (Psalm 117:10)

℟. God is the Lord...

℣. And this came about from the Lord, and it is wonderful in our eyes. (Psalm 117:23)

℟. God is the Lord...

The Apolytikia & Theotokion

Then the Choirs chant the APOLYTIKIA (Dismissal Hymns) according to the order prescribed in the Typikon, along with its corresponding THEOTOKION in the same mode.

Kathismata

After the designated reading of the Psalter, or in its absence, the Priest says the SMALL LITANY:

The Small Litany

Again and again, in peace, let us pray to the Lord. ℟. Lord, have mercy. *(after each)*

Help us, save us, have mercy on us, and protect us, O God, by Your grace. ℟.

Commemorating our most holy, pure, blessed, and glorious Lady, the Theotokos and ever-virgin Mary, with all the saints, let us commend ourselves and one another and our whole life to Christ our God. ℟. To You, O Lord.

PRIEST:

For Yours is the dominion, and Yours is the kingdom and the power and the glory, of the Father and of the Son and of the Holy Spirit, now and forever and to the ages of ages. ℟. Amen.

*The Choirs chant the Sessional Hymns (*KATHISMATA*) according to their prescribed order. Preceding the 2nd hymn is a psalmic verse.*

The Verses for the 2nd Hymn of the Kathisma Monday and Tuesday.

FOR THE 1ST SET.

℣. O Lord, do not reprove me in Your anger, nor discipline me in Your wrath. (Psalm 6:2)

FOR THE 2ND SET.

℣. Look upon me and have mercy on me, according to the judgment of those who love Your name. (Psalm 118:132)

FOR THE 3RD SET.

℣. God is wondrous in His saints. (Psalm 67:36)

Wednesday and Friday.

FOR THE 1ST SET.

℣. Exalt the Lord our God, and worship at the footstool of His feet; for He is holy. (Psalm 98:5)

FOR THE 2ND SET.

℣. God is our king before the ages; He worked salvation in the midst of the earth. (Psalm 73:12)

FOR THE 3RD SET.

℣. God is wondrous in His saints. (Psalm 67:36)

Thursday.

FOR THE 1ST SET.

℣. Their proclamation went forth into all the earth, and their words to the ends of the world. (Psalm 18:5)

FOR THE 2ND SET.

℣. The heavens declare the glory of God; the firmament shows the creation of His hands. (Psalm 18:2)

FOR THE 3RD SET.

℣. God is wondrous in His saints. (Psalm 67:36)

Saturday. For the Martyrs.

℣. God is wondrous in His saints. (Psalm 67:36)

℣. To the saints on His earth has the Lord been wondrous. (Psalm 15:3)

Saturday. For the Reposed.

℣. Blessed are they whom You have chosen and received, O Lord. (Psalm 64:5)

℣. Their souls shall dwell among good things. (Psalm 24:13)

The 50th Psalm
PROESTOS (OR READER):

Have mercy on me, O God, according to Your great mercy; and according to the abundance of Your compassion, blot out my transgression.

Wash me thoroughly from my lawlessness and cleanse me from my sin.

For I know my lawlessness, and my sin is always before me.

Against You only have I sinned and done evil in Your sight; that You may be justified in Your words, and overcome when You are judged.

For behold, I was conceived in transgressions, and in sins my mother bore me.

Behold, You love truth; You showed me the unknown and secret things of Your wisdom.

You shall sprinkle me with hyssop, and I will be cleansed; You shall wash me, and I will be made whiter than snow.

You shall make me hear joy and gladness; my bones that were humbled shall greatly rejoice.

Turn Your face from my sins, and blot out all my transgressions.

Create in me a clean heart, O God, and renew a right spirit within me.

Do not cast me away from Your presence, and do not take Your Holy Spirit from me.

Restore to me the joy of Your salvation, and uphold me with Your guiding Spirit.

I will teach transgressors Your ways, and the ungodly shall turn back to You.

Deliver Me from bloodguiltiness, O God, the God of my salvation, and my tongue shall greatly rejoice in Your righteousness.

O Lord, You shall open my lips, and my mouth will declare Your praise.

For if You desired sacrifice, I would give it; You will not be pleased with whole burnt offerings.

A sacrifice to God is a broken spirit, a broken and humble heart God will not despise.

Do good, O Lord, in Your good pleasure to Zion, and let the walls of Jerusalem be built.

Then You will be pleased with a sacrifice of righteousness, with offerings and whole burnt offerings.

Then shall they offer young bulls on Your altar.

If the CANONS will not be chanted, then straightway read the KONTAKION and SYNAXARION continued on page 132.

⋘⋘⋘⋘⋘

Otherwise the Choirs proceed as follows:
The Canons
After the 3rd Ode, the Priest says the SMALL LITANY.

The Small Litany
Again and again, in peace, let us pray to the Lord. ℟. Lord, have mercy. (after each)

Help us, save us, have mercy on us, and protect us, O God, by Your grace. ℟.

Commemorating our most holy, pure, blessed, and glorious Lady, the Theotokos and ever-virgin Mary, with all the saints, let us commend ourselves and one another and our whole life to Christ our God. ℟. To You, O Lord.

PRIEST:
For You are our God, and to You we give glory, to the Father, the Son and the Holy Spirit, now and forever and to the ages of ages. ℟. Amen.

The Choirs chant the Mid-Ode Kathismata, and immediately following the Heirmos of the 6th Ode, again the Priest says the SMALL LITANY.

The Small Litany

Again and again, in peace, let us pray to the Lord. ℟ Lord, have mercy. (after each)

Help us, save us, have mercy on us, and protect us, O God, by Your grace. ℟

Commemorating our most holy, pure, blessed, and glorious Lady, the Theotokos and ever-virgin Mary, with all the saints, let us commend ourselves and one another and our whole life to Christ our God. ℟ To You, O Lord.

PRIEST:

For You are the King of peace and the Savior of our souls, and to You we offer up glory, to the Father and the Son and the Holy Spirit, now and forever and to the ages of ages. ℟ Amen.

The Kontakion & Synaxarion

And the Reader recites the KONTAKION and SYNAXARION.

After this, to complete the CANONS, the Choirs chant the Heirmos of the 8th Ode, preceded by the verse:

℣. We praise and we bless and we worship the Lord.

Following the Heirmos of the 8th Ode, the Priest announces the ODE OF THE THEOTOKOS and proceeds to cense the entire church.

The Ode of the Theotokos
PRIEST:

Let us honor and magnify in song the Theotokos and the Mother of the light.

And the following verses of the ODE OF THE THEOTOKOS (Luke 1:46-55) are chanted by the Choirs.

℣. My soul magnifies the Lord, and my spirit has rejoiced in God my Savior.

MORE honorable than the Cherubim, and beyond compare more glorious than the Seraphim, without corruption you gave birth to God the Logos. We magnify you, the true Theotokos. (and so after each of the following verses.)

℣. For He has looked upon the humble state of His handmaid; for behold, from now on, all generations will call me blessed. ℟.

℣. For He who is mighty has done great things for me, and holy is His name, and His mercy is for generations of generations on those who fear Him. ℟.

℣. He has shown strength with His arm; He has scattered the proud in the imagination of their hearts. ℟.

℣. He has put down the mighty from their thrones, and exalted the humble. He has filled the hungry with good things, and He has sent the rich away empty. ℟.

℣. He has helped Israel His servant in remembrance of His mercy, as He spoke to our fathers, to Abraham and to his seed forever. ℟.

And the Choirs continue with chanting the 9th Ode of the CANON and its Heirmos.

Following the Heirmos *of the 9th Ode, the Choirs chant the* MEGALYNARION OF THE THEOTOKOS.

The Megalynarion of the Theotokos
IT is truly right to bless you, Theotokos, ever-blessed, most pure and the Mother of our God.

MORE honorable than the Cherubim, and beyond compare more glorious than the Seraphim, without corruption you gave birth to God the Logos. We magnify you, the true Theotokos.

Then the Priest says the SMALL LITANY.

The Small Litany
Again and again, in peace, let us pray to the Lord. ℟. Lord, have mercy. (after each)

Help us, save us, have mercy on us, and protect us, O God, by Your grace. ℟.

Commemorating our most holy, pure, blessed, and glorious Lady, the Theotokos and ever-virgin Mary, with all the saints, let us commend ourselves and one another and our whole life to Christ our God. ℟ To You, O Lord.

PRIEST:

For all the powers of heaven praise You, and to You we offer up glory, to the Father, the Son and the Holy Spirit, now and forever and to the ages of ages. ℟ Amen.

The Exapostilarion

The Choirs chant the designated EXAPOSTILARION with its corresponding Theotokion.

The Praises

After the EXAPOSTILARION, the PRAISES are chanted (as on page 94) along with the designated Stichera for the day, if there are any.

Otherwise, if there are no verses prescribed for the day, then the 3 psalms (148, 149, 150) are read, beginning with Praise the Lord from the heavens… as shown on page 137.

READER:
Psalm 148

Praise the Lord from the heavens, praise Him in the highest.

Praise Him, all you His angels; praise Him, all you His hosts.

Praise Him, sun and moon; praise Him, all you stars and light.

Praise Him, you heavens of heavens, and you waters above the heavens. Let them praise the Lord's name.

For He spoke, and they were made; He commanded, and they were created.

He established them forever and unto ages of ages; He set forth His ordinance, and it shall not pass away.

Praise the Lord from the earth, you dragons and all the deeps,

Fire and hail, snow and ice, stormy wind, which perform His word.

Mountains and all the hills, fruitful trees and all cedars,

Wild animals and all cattle, creeping things and flying birds,

Kings of the earth and all peoples, princes and all judges of the earth.

Young men and maidens, elders with younger; let them praise the Lord's name, for His name alone is exalted.

His thanksgiving is in earth and heaven. And He shall exalt the horn of His people.

A hymn for all His saints, for the children of Israel, a people who draw near to Him.

Psalm 149

Sing to the Lord a new song, His praise in the assembly of His holy ones.

Let Israel be glad in Him who made him, and let the children of Zion greatly rejoice in their King.

Let them praise His name with dance; with tambourine and harp let them sing to Him;

For the Lord is pleased with His people, and He shall exalt the gentle with salvation.

The holy ones shall boast in glory, and they shall greatly rejoice on their beds.

The high praise of God shall be in their mouth and a two-edged sword in their hand.

To deal retribution to the nations, reproving among the peoples.

To shackle their kings with chains and

their nobles with fetters of iron.

To fulfill among them the written judgment: this glory have all His holy ones.

Psalm 150

Praise God in His saints; praise Him in the firmament of His power.

Praise Him for His mighty acts; praise Him according to the abundance of His greatness.

Praise Him with the sound of a trumpet; praise Him with the harp and lyre;

Praise Him with timbrel and dance; praise Him with strings and flute;

Praise Him with resounding cymbals; praise Him with triumphant cymbals; Let everything that breathes praise the Lord.

Glory to the Father and to the Son and to the Holy Spirit.

Both now and forever and to the ages of ages. Amen.

And straightway after the PRAISES, the SMALL DOXOLOGY is read.

The Small Doxology
PROESTOS (OR READER):

To You is due glory, O Lord our God, and to You we offer up glory, to the Father and to the Son and to the Holy Spirit, both now and forever and to the ages of ages. Amen.

Glory to God in the highest, and on earth peace, goodwill among men.

We praise You, we bless You, we worship You, we glorify You, we give thanks to You for Your great glory.

O Lord, King, O heavenly God, the Father Almighty, O Lord the only-begotten Son, O Jesus Christ, and the Holy Spirit.

O Lord, God, Lamb of God, Son of the Father, who take away the sin of the world: have mercy on us, You who take away the sins of the world.

Receive our prayer, You who sit at the right hand of the Father, and have mercy on us.

For You alone are holy; You alone are Lord, Jesus Christ, to the glory of God the Father. Amen.

FOR DAILY CELEBRATION

Every day I will bless You, and I will praise Your name forever and unto the ages of ages.

O Lord, You have been our refuge from generation to generation. I said: O Lord, have mercy on me; heal my soul, for I have sinned against You.

O Lord, to You have I fled for refuge; teach me to do Your will, for You are my God.

For in You is the fountain of life; in Your light we shall see light.

Continue Your mercy unto those who know You.

O Lord, keep us this day without sin.

Blessed are You, O Lord, God of our fathers, and praised and glorified is Your name unto the ages. Amen.

O Lord, let Your mercy be upon us for we have set our hope in You.

Blessed are You, O Lord, teach me Your commandments.

Blessed are You, O Master, grant me understanding of Your commandments.

Blessed are You, O Holy One, enlighten me with Your commandments.

O Lord, Your mercy is forever. Do not despise the works of Your hands.

To You is due praise, to You is due song, to You is due glory, to the Father and to the Son and to the Holy Spirit, now and forever and to the ages of ages. Amen.

The Litany of Completion
PRIEST:

LET us complete our morning prayer to the Lord.

℟. Lord, have mercy. (for first two petitions)

Help us, save us, have mercy on us, and protect us, O God, by Your grace. ℟.

That the whole day may be perfect, holy, peaceful, and sinless, let us ask the Lord.

℟. Grant this, O Lord. (after each petition)

For an angel of peace, a faithful guide, a guardian of our souls and bodies, let us ask the Lord. ℟.

For pardon and remission of our sins and transgressions, let us ask the Lord. ℟.

For that which is good and beneficial for our souls, and for peace for the world, let us ask the Lord. ℟.

That we may complete the remaining

time of our life in peace and repentance, let us ask the Lord. ℟.

And let us ask for a Christian end to our life, peaceful, without shame and suffering, and for a good defense before the awesome judgment seat of Christ. ℟.

Commemorating our most holy, pure, blessed, and glorious Lady, the Theotokos and ever-virgin Mary, with all the saints, let us commend ourselves and one another and our whole life to Christ our God. ℟. To You, O Lord.

PRIEST:

For You are a God of mercy and compassion who loves mankind, and to You we give glory, to the Father and to the Son and to the Holy Spirit, now and forever and to the ages of ages. ℟. Amen.

And the Priest turns to face the people in order to offer them a blessing of peace.

Peace be with all. ℟. And with your spirit.

PRIEST: Let us bow our heads to the Lord. ℟. To You, O Lord.

The Prayer at the Bowing of the Heads
PRIEST:

O HOLY Lord, who dwell on high and watch over the lowly, and who with Your all-seeing eye look upon all creation, to You have we bowed the neck of our soul and body, and we entreat You, O Holy of Holies: Stretch forth Your invisible hand from Your holy dwelling place and bless us all; and if in any way we have sinned, whether voluntarily or involuntarily, pardon us, as You are a good God and love mankind, granting us Your good things in this world and in the world to come.

Then the Priest exclaims:

For Yours it is to show mercy and to save us, O our God, and to You we offer up glory, to the Father and to the Son and to the Holy Spirit, now and forever and to ages of ages. ℟. Amen.

The Aposticha

The APOSTICHA hymns are chanted with the following verses, unless others are otherwise provided.

Monday, Tuesday, Wednesday, and Friday.

℣. We were filled with Your mercy in the morning, and in all our days we greatly rejoiced and were glad; gladden us in return for the days You humbled us, for the years we saw evil things. And behold Your servants and Your works, and guide their sons. (89:14-16)

℣. And let the brightness of the Lord our God be upon us, and prosper for us the works of our hands, yes, prosper for us the work of our hands. (89:17)

Thursday.

℣. The heavens declare the glory of God; the firmament shows the creation of His hands. (18:2)

℣. To the saints on His earth has the Lord been wondrous. (15:3)

Saturday. For the Martyrs and Reposed.

℣. God is wondrous in His saints. (67:36)

℣. To the saints on His earth has the Lord been wondrous. (15:3)

℣. Blessed are they whom You have chosen and received, O Lord. (64:5)

The Theotokion (or Stavrotheotokion on Wednesday and Friday mornings) is chanted here, preceded by the Glory; both now.

PROESTOS (OR PRIEST):

IT is good to give thanks to the Lord and to sing to Your name, O Most High. To proclaim Your mercy in the morning and Your truth at night.

The Trisagion & Lord's Prayer
READER:

HOLY God, Holy Mighty, Holy Immortal, have mercy on us. (3)

Glory to the Father and to the Son and to the Holy Spirit. Both now and forever and to the ages of ages. Amen.

All-holy Trinity, have mercy on us, Lord, forgive our sins. Master, pardon our transgressions. Holy One, visit and heal our infirmities, for Your name's sake.

Lord, have mercy. (3)

Glory to the Father and to the Son and to the Holy Spirit. Both now and forever and to the ages of ages. Amen.

Our Father, who art in heaven, hallowed be Thy name. Thy kingdom come, Thy will be done on earth as it is in heaven. Give us this day our daily bread, and forgive us our trespasses as we forgive those who trespass against us. And lead us not into temptation, but deliver us from evil.

PRIEST:

For Thine is the kingdom and the power and the glory, of the Father and of the Son and of the Holy Spirit, now and forever and to the ages of ages. ℟ Amen.

The Apolytikion & Theotokion

Then the Choir chants the APOLYTIKION of the day with its corresponding THEOTOKION.

In the parishes today, when the Divine Liturgy will not be celebrated, the reading of the EPISTLE and GOSPEL of the day takes place immediately following the APOLYTIKIA. Then proceed to the SUPPLICATIONS and DISMISSAL.

The Epistle

PRIEST: Let us be attentive.

The Reader intones the Prokeimenon.

PRIEST: Wisdom.

READER: The reading is from (title).

PRIEST: Let us be attentive.

The Reader reads Epistle selection.

PRIEST: Peace to you. ℟ Alleluia. Alleluia. Alleluia.

The Gospel

PRIEST: Wisdom. Arise. Let us hear the holy Gospel. Peace be with all. ℟ And with your spirit.

PRIEST: The reading is from the Holy Gospel according to (name). Let us be attentive.

CHOIR: Glory to You, O Lord, glory to You.

The Priest reads the designated GOSPEL.

CHOIR: Glory to You, O Lord, glory to You.

※※※※※

If the Divine Liturgy will be celebrated, the SUPPLICATIONS *and* DISMISSAL *are said quietly by the Priest ahead of the service. Otherwise, continue as below.*

The Supplications
PRIEST:

Have mercy on us, O God, according to Your great mercy, we pray You, hear us and have mercy.

℟. Lord, have mercy. (3)

Again we pray for pious and Orthodox Christians. ℟.

Again we pray for our Archbishop (name). ℟.

Again we pray for our brethren: the priests, the hieromonks, the deacons, the monastics, and all our brotherhood in Christ. ℟.

Again we pray for mercy, life, peace, health, salvation, protection, forgiveness, and remission of the sins of the servants of God, all pious Orthodox Christians residing and visiting the city: the parishioners, the members of the parish council, the stewards, and benefactors of this holy church. ℟.

Again we pray for the blessed and ever-memorable founders of this holy church, and for all our fathers and brethren who have fallen asleep before us, who here have been piously laid to their rest, as well as the Orthodox everywhere. ℟.

Again we pray for those who bear fruit and do good works in this holy and all-venerable church, for those who labor and those who sing, and for the people here present who await Your great and rich mercy. ℟.

PRIEST:

For You are a merciful God and love mankind, and to You we offer up glory, to the Father and to the Son and to the Holy Spirit, now and forever and to the ages of ages. ℟. Amen.

Following the SUPPLICATIONS, the Priest proclaims: Wisdom. ℟. Give the blessing.

PRIEST:

Blessed is He who is, Christ our God, always, now and forever and to the ages of ages. ℟. Amen.

PROESTOS (OR READER):

May the Lord God strengthen the holy and pure faith of devout and Orthodox Christians, together with His holy Church, and this city, unto the ages of ages. ℟. Amen.

PRIEST:

Glory to You, Christ God, our hope, glory to You.

READER:

Glory to the Father and to the Son and to the Holy Spirit. Both now and forever and to the ages of ages. Amen. Lord, have mercy (3). Holy Father, give the blessing.

The Great Dismissal

Now the Priest does the GREAT DISMISSAL. If it is an afterfeast of the Master, begin with its characteristic phrase. Otherwise as follows:

MAY Christ our true God, through the intercessions of His all-pure and all-immaculate holy Mother; the power of the precious and life-giving Cross; the protection of the honorable, bodiless powers of heaven; the supplications of the honorable, glorious prophet and forerunner John the Baptist; of the holy, glorious, and praiseworthy apostles; of the holy, glorious, and triumphant martyrs; of our righteous and God-bearing Fathers; of (the saint of the church); of the holy and righteous ancestors of God Joachim and Anna; of (the saint of the day), whose memory we celebrate; and of all the saints; have mercy on us and save us, for He is good and loves mankind.

Through the prayers of our holy fathers, Lord Jesus Christ, our God, have mercy on us. ℟. Amen.

THE SERVICE OF
DAILY ORTHROS
for the Great 40 Days of the Fast

PRIEST:

BLESSED is our God always, now and forever and to the ages of ages. ℟. Amen.

Glory to You, our God, glory to You.

O HEAVENLY King, O Comforter, the Spirit of Truth, who are present everywhere and filling all things, the treasury of good things and giver of life: O come and abide in us, and cleanse us from every stain, and save our souls, O Good one.

On Monday of the 1st week of the Fast, after the Blessing is said, the Priest censes crosswise around the Holy Altar, as the TRISAGION is read. Omit the Save, O Lord, Your people, etc.

The reader says: **Lord, have mercy** (12). **In the name of the Lord, Father give the blessing.** The Priest exclaims: **Glory to the holy and consubstantial...**, and the reading of the SIX PSALMS begins.

Otherwise, on all other weekdays of the Fast, continue as normal.

The Trisagion & Lord's Prayer
READER:

Holy God, Holy Mighty, Holy Immortal, have mercy on us. (3)

Glory to the Father and to the Son and to the Holy Spirit. Both now and forever and to the ages of ages. Amen.

All-holy Trinity, have mercy on us, Lord, forgive our sins. Master, pardon our transgressions. Holy One, visit and heal our infirmities, for Your name's sake.

Lord, have mercy. (3)

Glory to the Father and to the Son and to the Holy Spirit. Both now and forever and to the ages of ages. Amen.

FOR THE LENTEN FAST

OUR Father, who art in heaven, hallowed be Thy name. Thy kingdom come, Thy will be done on earth as it is in heaven. Give us this day our daily bread, and forgive us our trespasses as we forgive those who trespass against us. And lead us not into temptation, but deliver us from evil.

PRIEST:

For Thine is the kingdom and the power and the glory, of the Father and of the Son and of the Holy Spirit, now and forever and to the ages of ages. ℟. Amen.

The Troparia
READER:

SAVE, O Lord, Your people and bless Your inheritance. Grant victory to the faithful against the adversaries of the faith, and protect Your people by the power of Your Cross.

Glory to the Father and to the Son and to the Holy Spirit.

You who were raised upon the Cross with volition, grant to Your new community Your compassion, which bears its name in Your honor, O Christ our God; gladden now with all Your strength, O Lord, our faithful leaders believing, granting them all victories against opponents competing; may they have as an alliance with You, the weapon of peace, the trophy invincible.

Both now and forever and to the ages of ages. Amen.

O PROTECTION unashamed and most formidable, do not despise, O good one, any of our petitions, all-praised Lady Theotokos: Strengthen now the Orthodox community, save those whom you have elected to lead us, and supply them with victory from the heavenly heights; for you have given birth unto God, and you alone are blessed.

PRIEST:

HAVE mercy on us, O God, according to Your great mercy, we pray You, hear us and have mercy.

℟. Lord, have mercy. (3, after each petition)

Let us pray for pious and Orthodox Christians. ℟.

Again we pray for our Archbishop (name). ℟.

PRIEST:

For You are a merciful God who loves mankind, and to You we offer up glory, to the Father and to the Son and to the Holy Spirit, now and forever and to the ages of ages. ℟. Amen.

READER:

In the name of the Lord, Father give the blessing.

PRIEST:

GLORY to the holy and consubstantial, and life-giving, and undivided Trinity always, now and forever and to the ages of ages. ℟. Amen.

The Six Psalms

READER:

GLORY to God in the highest, and on earth peace, goodwill among men. (3)

O Lord, You shall open my lips, and my mouth will declare Your praise. (2)

Psalm 3

O LORD, why do those who afflict me multiply?

Many are those who rise up against me.

Many are those who say to my soul, "There is no salvation for him in his God."

But You, O Lord, are my protector, my glory and the One who lifts up my head.

I cried to the Lord with my voice, and He heard me from His holy hill.

I lay down and slept; I awoke, for the Lord will help me.

I will not be afraid of ten thousands of people who set themselves against me all around.

Arise, O Lord, and save me, O my God, for You struck all those who were foolishly at enmity with me; You broke the teeth of sinners.

Salvation is of the Lord, and Your blessing is upon Your people.

(and again)

I lay down and slept; I awoke, for the Lord will help me.

Psalm 37

O LORD, do not rebuke me in Your wrath, nor chasten me in Your anger.

For Your arrows are fixed in me, and Your hand rests on me.

There is no healing in my flesh because of Your wrath; there is no peace in my bones because of my sins.

For my transgressions rise up over my head; like a heavy burden they are heavy on me.

My wounds grow foul and fester because of my folly.

I suffer misery, and I am utterly bowed down; I go all the day long with a sad face.

For my loins are filled with mockeries, and there is no healing in my flesh.

I am afflicted and greatly humbled; I roar because of the groaning of my heart.

O Lord, all my desire is before You, and

my groaning is not hidden from You.

My heart is troubled; my strength fails me, and the light of my eyes, even this is not with me.

My friends and neighbors draw near and stand against me, and my near of kin stand far off;

And those who seek my soul use violence, and those who seek evil for me speak folly; and they meditate on deceit all the day long.

But I like a deaf man do not hear, and I am like a mute who does not open his mouth.

I am like a man who does not hear, and who has no reproofs in his mouth.

For in You, O Lord, I hope; You will hear, O Lord my God.

For I said, "Let not my enemies rejoice over me, for when my foot was shaken, they boasted against me."

For I am ready for wounds, and my pain is continually with me.

For I will declare my transgression, and I will be anxious about my sin.

But my enemies live, and are become stronger than I; and those who hate me unjustly are multiplied;

Those who repaid me evil for good slandered me, because I pursue righteousness;

Do not forsake me, O Lord; O my God, do not depart from me;

Give heed to help me, O Lord of my salvation.

(and again)

Do not forsake me, O Lord; O my God, do not depart from me;

Give heed to help me, O Lord of my salvation.

Psalm 62

O GOD, my God, I rise early to be with You; my soul thirsts for You.

How often my flesh thirsts for You in a desolate, impassable, and waterless land.

So in the holy place I appear before You, to see Your power and Your glory.

Because Your mercy is better than life, my lips shall praise You.

Thus I will bless You in my life; I will lift up my hands in Your name.

May my soul be filled, as if with marrow

and fatness, and my mouth shall sing praise to You with lips filled with rejoicing.

If I remembered You on my bed, I meditated on You at daybreak;

For You are my helper, and in the shelter of Your wings I will greatly rejoice.

My soul follows close behind You; Your right hand takes hold of me.

But they seek for my soul in vain; they shall go into the lowest parts of the earth. They shall be given over to the edge of the sword; they shall be a portion for foxes.

But the king shall be glad in God; all who swear by Him shall be praised, for the mouth that speaks unrighteous things is stopped.

(and again)

I meditated on You at daybreak; For You are my helper, and in the shelter of Your wings I will greatly rejoice.

My soul follows close behind You; Your right hand takes hold of me.

Glory to the Father and to the Son and to the Holy Spirit, both now and forever and to the ages of ages. Amen.

Alleluia, alleluia, alleluia; glory to You, O God. (3)

Lord, have mercy. (3)

Glory to the Father and to the Son and to the Holy Spirit, both now and forever and to the ages of ages. Amen.

Psalm 87

O Lord God of my salvation, I cry day and night before You.

Let my prayer come before You; incline Your ear to my supplication, O Lord.

For my soul is filled with sorrows, and my soul draws near to Hades;

I am counted among those who go down into the pit; I am like a helpless man, free among the dead;

Like slain men thrown down and sleeping in a grave, whom You remember no more, but they are removed from Your hand.

They laid me in the lowest pit, in dark places and in the shadow of death.

Your wrath rested upon me, and You brought all Your billows over me.

You removed my acquaintances far from me; they made me an abomination among themselves;

I was betrayed, and did not go forth. My eyes weakened from poverty;

O Lord, I cry to You the whole day long; I spread out my hands to You.

Will You work wonders for the dead? Or will physicians raise them up, and acknowledge You?

Shall anyone in the grave describe Your mercy and Your truth in destruction?

Shall Your wonders be known in darkness, and Your righteousness in a forgotten land?

But I cry to You, O Lord, and in the morning my prayer shall come near to You.

Why, O Lord, do You reject my soul, and turn away Your face from me?

I am poor and in troubles from my youth; but having been exalted, I was humbled and brought into despair.

Your fierce anger passed over me, and Your terrors greatly troubled me;

They compassed me like water all the day long; they surrounded me at once.

You removed far from me neighbor and friend, and my acquaintances because of my misery.

(and again)

O Lord God of my salvation, I cry day and night before You.

Let my prayer come before You; incline Your ear to my supplication, O Lord.

Psalm 102

BLESS the Lord, O my soul, and everything within me, bless His holy name.

Bless the Lord, O my soul, and forget not all His rewards:

Who is merciful to all your transgressions, who heals all your diseases,

Who redeems your life from corruption, who crowns you with mercy and compassion,

Who satisfies your desire with good things; and your youth is renewed like the eagle's.

The Lord shows mercies and judgment to all who are wronged.

He made known His ways to Moses, the

things He willed to the sons of Israel.

The Lord is compassionate and merciful, slow to anger, and abounding in mercy. He will not become angry to the end, nor will He be wrathful forever;

He did not deal with us according to our sins, nor reward us according to our transgressions;

For according to the height of heaven from earth, so the Lord reigns in mercy over those who fear Him;

As far as the east is from the west, so He removes our transgressions from us.

As a father has compassion on his children, so the Lord has compassion on those who fear Him, for He knows how He formed us; He remembers we are dust.

As for man, his days are like grass, as a flower of the field, so he flourishes;

For the wind passes through it, and it shall not remain; and it shall no longer know its place.

But the mercy of the Lord is from age to age upon those who fear Him,

And His righteousness upon children's children, to such as keep His covenant and remember His commandments, to do them.

The Lord prepared His throne in heaven, and His Kingdom rules over all.

Bless the Lord, all you His angels, mighty in strength, who do His word, so as to hear the voice of His words.

Bless the Lord, all you His hosts, His ministers who do His will;

Bless the Lord, all His works, in all places of His dominion; Bless the Lord, O my soul.

(and again)

In all places of His dominion; Bless the Lord, O my soul.

Psalm 142

O LORD, hear my prayer; give ear to my supplication in Your truth; answer me in Your righteousness;

Do not enter into judgment with Your servant, for no one living shall become righteous in Your sight.

For the enemy persecuted my soul; he humbled my life to the ground;

He caused me to dwell in dark places as

one long dead, and my spirit was in anguish within me; my heart was troubled within me.

I remembered the days of old, and I meditated on all Your works; I meditated on the works of Your hands.

I spread out my hands to You; my soul thirsts for You like a waterless land.

Hear me speedily, O Lord; my spirit faints within me;

Turn not Your face from me, lest I become like those who go down into the pit.

Cause me to hear Your mercy in the morning, for I hope in You;

Make me know, O Lord, the way wherein I should walk, for I lift up my soul to You.

Deliver me from my enemies, O Lord, for to You I flee for refuge. Teach me to do Your will, for You are my God;

Your good Spirit shall guide me in the land of uprightness. For Your name's sake, O Lord, give me life;

In Your righteousness You shall bring my soul out of affliction. In Your mercy You shall destroy my enemies;

You shall utterly destroy all who afflict my soul, for I am Your servant.

(and again)

Answer me, O Lord, in Your righteousness, and do not enter into judgment with Your servant. (2)

Your good Spirit shall guide me in the land of uprightness.

Glory to the Father and to the Son and to the Holy Spirit, both now and forever and to the ages of ages. Amen.

Alleluia, alleluia, alleluia; glory to You, O God. (3) Our hope, O Lord, glory to You.

The Litany of Peace
PRIEST:

IN peace, let us pray to the Lord.
℟. Lord, have mercy. (after each petition)

For the peace from above and for the salvation of our souls, let us pray to the Lord. ℟.

For the peace of the whole world, for the stability of the holy churches of God, and for the unity of all, let us pray to the Lord. ℟.

For this holy house and for those who enter it with faith, reverence, and the fear of God, let us pray to the Lord. ℟.

For pious and Orthodox Christians, let us pray to the Lord. ℟.

For our Archbishop (name), for the honorable presbyterate, for the diaconate in Christ, and for all the clergy and the people, let us pray to the Lord. ℟.

For our country, for the president, and for all in public service, let us pray to the Lord. ℟.

For this city, and for every city and land, and for the faithful who live in them, let us pray to the Lord. ℟.

For favorable weather, for an abundance of the fruits of the earth, and for peaceful times, let us pray to the Lord. ℟.

For those who travel by land, sea, and air, for the sick, the suffering, the captives and for their salvation, let us pray to the Lord. ℟.

For our deliverance from all affliction, wrath, danger, and necessity, let us pray to the Lord. ℟.

Help us, save us, have mercy on us, and protect us, O God, by Your grace. ℟.

Commemorating our most holy, pure, blessed, and glorious Lady, the Theotokos and ever-virgin Mary, with all the saints, let us commend ourselves and one another and our whole life to Christ our God. ℟. To You, O Lord.

PRIEST:

For to You belong all glory, honor, and worship, to the Father and to the Son and to the Holy Spirit, now and forever and to the ages of ages. ℟. Amen.

The Alleluias

After the LITANY OF PEACE, instead of the GOD IS THE LORD, the ALLELUIAS are chanted as follows:

CHOIRS:

℣. My spirit rises early in the morning to You, O God, for Your commands are a light upon the earth. (Isaiah 26:9)

℟. Alleluia. Alleluia. Alleluia.

℣. Learn righteousness, you who dwell on the earth. (Isaiah 26:9)

℟. Alleluia. Alleluia. Alleluia.

℣. Jealousy will seize an untaught people; and now fire will devour the adversaries. (Isaiah 26:11)

℟. Alleluia. Alleluia. Alleluia.

℣. Bring more evils on them, O Lord, bring more evils on them, on the glorious of the earth. (Isaiah 26:15)

℟. Alleluia. Alleluia. Alleluia.

The Hymns to the Trinity

And straightway the HYMNS TO THE TRINITY are chanted, each of which with the words Holy, holy, holy are You, our God, supplemented by the following:

Monday.

Through the intercessions of the Bodiless Hosts, save us.

Tuesday.

Through the intercessions of the Forerunner, save us.

Wednesday and Friday.

Through the power of Your Cross, save us.

Thursday.

Through the intercessions of the Apostles, save us.

The 2nd is with the characteristic phrase for the saint of the temple: Through the intercessions of the Hierarch… (or of the venerable one or of the prizewinner etc.), save us.

But if the temple is honored with the name of the Holy Trinity or of our Lord Jesus Christ, or the Theotokos, supplement the 2nd as the 1st. But for Thursday supplement with the Through the intercessions of the Hierarch… for Saint Nicholas. If the temple is honored with the name of the precious Cross, supplement with the Through the power of Your Cross…

The 3rd is always with the phrase: Through the Theotokos, have mercy on us.

Kathismata of the Psalter

After the HYMNS TO THE TRINITY are chanted, the assigned KATHISMATA OF THE PSALTER is read.

Following the designated reading of the Psalter, or in its absence, the Priest says the SMALL LITANY.

The Small Litany

Again and again, in peace, let us pray to the Lord. ℟. Lord, have mercy. (after each)

Help us, save us, have mercy on us, and protect us, O God, by Your grace. ℟.

Commemorating our most holy, pure, blessed, and glorious Lady, the Theotokos and ever-virgin Mary, with all the saints, let us commend ourselves and one another and our whole life to Christ our God. ℟. To You, O Lord.

PRIEST:

For Yours is the dominion, and Yours is the kingdom and the power and the glory, of the Father and of the Son and of the Holy Spirit, now and forever and to the ages of ages. ℟. Amen.

Kathismata Hymns

Following the SMALL LITANY, the Choirs chant the Sessional Hymns (KATHISMATA) according to their order.

If the KATHISMATA OF THE PSALTER is read,

The 50th Psalm
PROESTOS (OR READER):

HAVE mercy on me, O God, according to Your great mercy; and according to the abundance of Your compassion, blot out my transgression.

Wash me thoroughly from my lawlessness and cleanse me from my sin.

For I know my lawlessness, and my sin is always before me.

Against You only have I sinned and done evil in Your sight; that You may be justified in Your words, and overcome when You are judged.

For behold, I was conceived in transgressions, and in sins my mother bore me.

Behold, You love truth; You showed me the unknown and secret things of Your wisdom.

You shall sprinkle me with hyssop, and I will be cleansed; You shall wash me, and I will be made whiter than snow.

You shall make me hear joy and gladness; my bones that were humbled shall greatly rejoice.

Turn Your face from my sins, and blot out all my transgressions.

Create in me a clean heart, O God, and renew a right spirit within me.

Do not cast me away from Your presence, and do not take Your Holy Spirit from me.

Restore to me the joy of Your salvation, and uphold me with Your guiding Spirit.

I will teach transgressors Your ways, and the ungodly shall turn back to You.

Deliver Me from bloodguiltiness, O God, the God of my salvation, and my tongue shall greatly rejoice in Your righteousness.

O Lord, You shall open my lips, and my mouth will declare Your praise.

For if You desired sacrifice, I would give it; You will not be pleased with whole burnt offerings.

A sacrifice to God is a broken spirit, a broken and humble heart God will not despise.

Do good, O Lord, in Your good pleasure to Zion, and let the walls of Jerusalem be built.

Then You will be pleased with a sacrifice of righteousness, with offerings and whole burnt offerings.

Then shall they offer young bulls on Your altar.

FOR THE LENTEN FAST

After the reading of the 50TH PSALM, the Priest says the following intercession:

O GOD, save Your people and bless Your inheritance; visit Your world with mercy and compassions; exalt the horn of the Orthodox Christians, and send down upon us Your abundant mercies; through the intercessions of our all-pure Lady the Theotokos and ever-virgin Mary; the power of the precious and life-giving Cross, the protection of the honorable, bodiless powers of heaven; the supplications of the honorable and glorious prophet and forerunner John the Baptist; of the holy, glorious, and praise-worthy apostles; our Fathers among the saints, the great hierarchs and ecumenical teachers, Basil the Great, Gregory the Theologian and John Chrysostom; Athanasios, Cyril, and John the Merciful, patriarchs of Alexandria; Nicholas, bishop of Myra, Spyridon, bishop of Trimythous, Nektarios of Pentapolis, the wonder-workers; the holy, glorious great martyrs George the Victorious, Demetrios the Myrobletes, Theodore the Teron, and Theodore the General, Menas the Wonderworker; the hieromartyrs Haralambos and Eleftherios; the holy, glorious, and victorious martyrs; the glorious great martyr and all-laudable Euphemia; the holy and glorious martyrs Thecla, Barbara, Anastasia, Katherine, Kyriake, Fotene, Marina, Paraskeve and Irene; of our holy God-bearing Fathers; (local patron saint); the holy and righteous ancestors of God Joachim and Anna; of (saint of the day) whose memory we celebrate; and of all Your saints. We beseech You, only merciful Lord, hear us sinners who pray to You and have mercy on us.

CHOIRS: Lord, have mercy. (12)

PRIEST:

Through the mercy, compassions, and benevolence of Your only-begotten Son, with whom You are blessed, together with Your all-holy, good and life-giving Spirit, now and forever and to the ages of ages. ℟. Amen.

Biblical Odes and Canons

The Choirs may proceed to offer the BIBLICAL ODES according to the schedule below. Following these, the CANONS may be chanted in their proper order, with the SMALL LITANY following the Heirmos of the 3rd and 6th Odes.

If these are not offered, proceed straightway to the reading of the HYMN FOR THE MARTYRS and SYNAXARION on page 181.

Monday.
1st, 8th, 9th (for Zacharias).

Tuesday.
2nd, 8th, 9th.

Wednesday.
3rd, 8th, 9th.

Thursday.
4th, 8th, 9th.

Friday.
5th, 8th, 9th.

After the 3rd Ode of the CANONS, *the Priest says the* SMALL LITANY.

The Small Litany

Again and again, in peace, let us pray to the Lord. ℟ Lord, have mercy. (after each)

Help us, save us, have mercy on us, and protect us, O God, by Your grace. ℟

Commemorating our most holy, pure, blessed, and glorious Lady, the Theotokos and ever-virgin Mary, with all the saints, let us commend ourselves and one another and our whole life to Christ our God. ℟ To You, O Lord.

PRIEST:

For You are our God, and to You we give glory, to the Father, the Son and the Holy Spirit, now and forever and to the ages of ages. ℟ Amen.

The Choirs chant the Mid-Ode Kathismata, followed by the Heirmos of the 6th Ode. Again the Priest says the SMALL LITANY.

The Small Litany

Again and again, in peace, let us pray to the Lord. ℟ Lord, have mercy. (after each)

Help us, save us, have mercy on us, and protect us, O God, by Your grace. ℟

Commemorating our most holy, pure, blessed, and glorious Lady, the Theotokos and ever-virgin Mary, with all the saints, let us commend ourselves and one another and our whole life to Christ our God. ℟ To You, O Lord.

PRIEST:

For You are the King of peace and the Savior of our souls, and to You we offer up glory, to the Father and the Son and the Holy Spirit, now and forever and to the ages of ages. ℟ Amen.

Hymn for the Martyrs and Synaxarion
The Reader now offers the reading of the HYMN FOR THE MARTYRS and SYNAXARION.

After this, to complete the CANONS, *the Choirs chant the* Heirmos *of the 8th Ode, preceded by the verse:*

℣. We praise and we bless and we worship the Lord.

Following the Heirmos *of the 8th Ode, the Priest announces the* ODE OF THE THEOTOKOS *and proceeds to cense the entire church.*

The Ode of the Theotokos

PRIEST:

Let us honor and magnify in song the Theotokos and the Mother of the light.

And the following verses of the ODE OF THE THEOTOKOS *(Luke 1:46-55) are chanted by the Choirs.*

℣. My soul magnifies the Lord, and my spirit has rejoiced in God my Savior.

MORE honorable than the Cherubim, and beyond compare more glorious than the Seraphim, without corruption you gave birth to God the Logos. We magnify you, the true Theotokos. *(and so after each of the following verses.)*

℣. For He has looked upon the humble state of His handmaid; for behold, from now on, all generations will call me blessed. ℟.

℣. For He who is mighty has done great things for me, and holy is His name, and His mercy is for generations of generations on those who fear Him. ℟.

℣. He has shown strength with His arm; He has scattered the proud in the imagination of their hearts. ℟.

℣. He has put down the mighty from their thrones, and exalted the humble. He has filled the hungry with good things, and He has sent the rich away empty. ℟.

℣. He has helped Israel His servant in remembrance of His mercy, as He spoke to our fathers, to Abraham and to his seed forever. ℟.

And the Choirs continue with chanting the 9th Ode of the CANON and its Heirmos.

Following the Heirmos of the 9th Ode, the Choirs chant the MEGALYNARION OF THE THEOTOKOS.

The Megalynarion of the Theotokos

IT is truly right to bless you, Theotokos, ever-blessed, most pure and the Mother of our God.

MORE honorable than the Cherubim, and beyond compare more glorious than the Seraphim, without corruption you gave birth to God the Logos. We magnify you, the true Theotokos.

Then the Priest says the SMALL LITANY.

The Small Litany

Again and again, in peace, let us pray to the Lord. ℟. Lord, have mercy. (after each)

Help us, save us, have mercy on us, and protect us, O God, by Your grace. ℟.

Commemorating our most holy, pure, blessed, and glorious Lady, the Theotokos and ever-virgin Mary, with all the saints, let us commend ourselves and one another and our whole life to Christ our God. ℟. To You, O Lord.

PRIEST:

For all the powers of heaven praise You, and to You we offer up glory, to the Father, the Son and the Holy Spirit, now and forever and to the ages of ages. ℟. Amen.

The Hymns of Light

The HYMNS OF LIGHT are chanted thrice, and as with the HYMNS TO THE TRINITY, each of set is supplemented with the following words:

Monday.

Through the intercessions of the Bodiless Hosts, and save me.

Tuesday.

Through the intercessions of the Forerunner, and save me.

Wednesday and Friday.

Through the power of Your Cross, and save me.

Thursday.

Through the intercessions of the Apostles, and save me.

The 2nd is with the characteristic phrase for the saint of the temple: Through the intercessions of the Hierarch… (or of the venerable one or of the prizewinner etc.), and save me.

But if the temple is honored with the name of the Holy Trinity or of our Lord Jesus Christ, or the Theotokos, supplement the 2nd as the 1st. But for Thursday supplement with the Through the intercessions of the Hierarch… for Saint Nicholas. If the temple is honored with the name of the precious Cross, supplement with the Through the power of Your Cross…

The 3rd is always with the phrase: Through the intercessions of the Theotokos, and save me.

The Praises

After the HYMNS OF LIGHT, the 3 psalms (148, 149, 150) of the PRAISES are are read, beginning with Praise the Lord from the heavens… as shown on page 187.

READER:

Psalm 148

PRAISE the Lord from the heavens, praise Him in the highest.

Praise Him, all you His angels; praise Him, all you His hosts.

Praise Him, sun and moon; praise Him, all you stars and light.

Praise Him, you heavens of heavens, and you waters above the heavens. Let them praise the Lord's name.

For He spoke, and they were made; He commanded, and they were created.

He established them forever and unto ages of ages; He set forth His ordinance, and it shall not pass away.

Praise the Lord from the earth, you dragons and all the deeps,

Fire and hail, snow and ice, stormy wind, which perform His word.

Mountains and all the hills, fruitful trees and all cedars,

Wild animals and all cattle, creeping things and flying birds,

Kings of the earth and all peoples, princes and all judges of the earth.

Young men and maidens, elders with younger; let them praise the Lord's name, for His name alone is exalted.

His thanksgiving is in earth and heaven. And He shall exalt the horn of His people.

A hymn for all His saints, for the children of Israel, a people who draw near to Him.

Psalm 149

Sing to the Lord a new song, His praise in the assembly of His holy ones.

Let Israel be glad in Him who made him, and let the children of Zion greatly rejoice in their King.

Let them praise His name with dance; with tambourine and harp let them sing to Him;

For the Lord is pleased with His people, and He shall exalt the gentle with salvation.

The holy ones shall boast in glory, and they shall greatly rejoice on their beds.

The high praise of God shall be in their mouth and a two-edged sword in their hand.

To deal retribution to the nations, reproving among the peoples.

To shackle their kings with chains and

their nobles with fetters of iron.

To fulfill among them the written judgment: this glory have all His holy ones.

Psalm 150

Praise God in His saints; praise Him in the firmament of His power.

Praise Him for His mighty acts; praise Him according to the abundance of His greatness.

Praise Him with the sound of a trumpet; praise Him with the harp and lyre;

Praise Him with timbrel and dance; praise Him with strings and flute;

Praise Him with resounding cymbals; praise Him with triumphant cymbals; Let everything that breathes praise the Lord.

Glory to the Father and to the Son and to the Holy Spirit.

Both now and forever and to the ages of ages. Amen.

And straightway after the PRAISES, the SMALL DOXOLOGY is read.

The Small Doxology
PROESTOS (OR READER):

To You is due glory, O Lord our God, and to You we offer up glory, to the Father and to the Son and to the Holy Spirit, both now and forever and to the ages of ages. Amen.

Glory to God in the highest, and on earth peace, goodwill among men.

We praise You, we bless You, we worship You, we glorify You, we give thanks to You for Your great glory.

O Lord, King, O heavenly God, the Father Almighty, O Lord the only-begotten Son, O Jesus Christ, and the Holy Spirit.

O Lord, God, Lamb of God, Son of the Father, who take away the sin of the world: have mercy on us, You who take away the sins of the world.

Receive our prayer, You who sit at the right hand of the Father, and have mercy on us.

For You alone are holy; You alone are Lord, Jesus Christ, to the glory of God the Father. Amen.

FOR THE LENTEN FAST

Every day I will bless You, and I will praise Your name forever and unto the ages of ages.

O Lord, You have been our refuge from generation to generation. I said: O Lord, have mercy on me; heal my soul, for I have sinned against You.

O Lord, to You have I fled for refuge; teach me to do Your will, for You are my God.

For in You is the fountain of life; in Your light we shall see light.

Continue Your mercy unto those who know You.

O Lord, keep us this day without sin.

Blessed are You, O Lord, God of our fathers, and praised and glorified is Your name unto the ages. Amen.

O Lord, let Your mercy be upon us for we have set our hope in You.

Blessed are You, O Lord, teach me Your commandments.

Blessed are You, O Master, grant me understanding of Your commandments.

Blessed are You, O Holy One, enlighten me with Your commandments.

O Lord, Your mercy is forever. Do not despise the works of Your hands.

To You is due praise, to You is due song, to You is due glory, to the Father and to the Son and to the Holy Spirit, now and forever and to the ages of ages. Amen.

The Litany of Completion
PRIEST:

LET us complete our morning prayer to the Lord.

℟. Lord, have mercy. (for first two petitions)

Help us, save us, have mercy on us, and protect us, O God, by Your grace. ℟.

That the whole day may be perfect, holy, peaceful, and sinless, let us ask the Lord.

℟. Grant this, O Lord. (after each petition)

For an angel of peace, a faithful guide, a guardian of our souls and bodies, let us ask the Lord. ℟.

For pardon and remission of our sins and transgressions, let us ask the Lord. ℟.

For that which is good and beneficial for our souls, and for peace for the world, let us ask the Lord. ℟.

That we may complete the remaining

time of our life in peace and repentance, let us ask the Lord. ℟.

And let us ask for a Christian end to our life, peaceful, without shame and suffering, and for a good defense before the awesome judgment seat of Christ. ℟.

Commemorating our most holy, pure, blessed, and glorious Lady, the Theotokos and ever-virgin Mary, with all the saints, let us commend ourselves and one another and our whole life to Christ our God. ℟. To You, O Lord.

PRIEST:

For You are a God of mercy and compassion who loves mankind, and to You we give glory, to the Father and to the Son and to the Holy Spirit, now and forever and to the ages of ages. ℟. Amen.

And the Priest turns to face the people in order to offer them a blessing of peace.

Peace be with all. ℟. And with your spirit.

PRIEST: Let us bow our heads to the Lord. ℟. To You, O Lord.

The Prayer at the Bowing of the Heads
PRIEST:

O HOLY Lord, who dwell on high and watch over the lowly, and who with Your all-seeing eye look upon all creation, to You have we bowed the neck of our soul and body, and we entreat You, O Holy of Holies: Stretch forth Your invisible hand from Your holy dwelling place and bless us all; and if in any way we have sinned, whether voluntarily or involuntarily, pardon us, as You are a good God and love mankind, granting us Your good things in this world and in the world to come.

Then the Priest exclaims:

For Yours it is to show mercy and to save us, O our God, and to You we offer up glory, to the Father and to the Son and to the Holy Spirit, now and forever and to ages of ages. ℟ Amen.

The Aposticha

The APOSTICHA hymns are chanted with the following verses.

℣. We were filled with Your mercy in the morning, and in all our days we greatly rejoiced and were glad; Gladden us in return for the days You humbled us, for the years we saw evil things. And behold Your servants and Your works, and guide their sons;. (89:14-16)

℣. And let the brightness of the Lord our God be upon us, and prosper for us the works of our hands, yes, prosper for us the work of our hands. (89:17)

The Theotokion (or Stavrotheotokion on Wednesday and Friday mornings) is chanted here, preceded by the Glory; both now.

PROESTOS (OR PRIEST):

IT is good to give thanks to the Lord and to sing to Your name, O Most High. To proclaim Your mercy in the morning and Your truth at night.

The Trisagion & Lord's Prayer
READER:

HOLY God, Holy Mighty, Holy Immortal, have mercy on us. (3)

Glory to the Father and to the Son and to the Holy Spirit. Both now and forever and to the ages of ages. Amen.

All-holy Trinity, have mercy on us, Lord, forgive our sins. Master, pardon our transgressions. Holy One, visit and heal our infirmities, for Your name's sake.

Lord, have mercy. (3)

Glory to the Father and to the Son and to the Holy Spirit. Both now and forever and to the ages of ages. Amen.

Our Father, who art in heaven, hallowed be Thy name. Thy kingdom come, Thy will be done on earth as it is in heaven. Give us this day our daily bread, and forgive us our trespasses as we forgive those who trespass against us. And lead us not into temptation, but deliver us from evil.

PRIEST:

For Thine is the kingdom and the power and the glory, of the Father and of the Son and of the Holy Spirit, now and forever and to the ages of ages. ℟. Amen.

The Troparion
READER:

Standing in the temple of your glory, we think we are standing in heaven: O Theotokos, O heavenly gate, open unto us the door of your mercy.

READER: Lord, have mercy. (40)

℣. Glory to the Father and to the Son and to the Holy Spirit. Both now and forever and to the ages of ages. Amen.

More honorable than the Cherubim, and beyond compare more glorious than the Seraphim, without corruption you gave birth to God the Logos. We magnify you, the true Theotokos.

READER:
In the name of the Lord, Father give the blessing.

PRIEST:
Blessed is He who is, Christ our God, always, now and forever and to the ages of ages. ℟. Amen.

PROESTOS (OR PRIEST):

O King of heaven, establish our rulers, strengthen the faith, calm the nations, make the world peaceful, protect this holy church and city, grant that our departed fathers and brethren may dwell with the righteous, and accept us in repentance and confession; for You are good and love mankind. ℟ Amen.

The Prayer of Saint Ephrem the Syrian

O LORD and Master of my life, give me not a spirit of sloth, vain curiosity, lust for power, and idle talk.

But give to me, Your servant, a spirit of prudence, humility, patience, and love.

Yes, O Lord and King, grant me to see my own faults and not to condemn my brother: for You are blessed to the ages of ages.

We make 12 small prostrations and one additional, repeating the final verse of the prayer.

Yes, O Lord and King, grant me to see my own faults and not to condemn my brother: for You are blessed to the ages of ages. Amen.

If the Hours will be read immediately after the Orthros, then begin here with the Come, let us worship…

Otherwise, proceed with the following GREAT DISMISSAL.

PRIEST:

Glory to You, Christ God, our hope, glory to You.

READER:

Glory to the Father and to the Son and to the Holy Spirit. Both now and forever and to the ages of ages. Amen. Lord, have mercy (3). Holy Father, give the blessing.

The Great Dismissal
PRIEST:

MAY Christ our true God, through the intercessions of His all-pure and all-immaculate holy Mother; the power of the precious and life-giving Cross; the protection of the honorable, bodiless powers of heaven; the supplications of the honorable, glorious prophet and forerunner John the Baptist; of the holy, glorious, and praiseworthy apostles;

of the holy, glorious, and triumphant martyrs; of our righteous and God-bearing Fathers; of (the saint of the church); of the holy and righteous ancestors of God Joachim and Anna; of (the saint of the day), whose memory we celebrate; and of all the saints; have mercy on us and save us, for He is good and loves mankind.

Through the prayers of our holy fathers, Lord Jesus Christ, our God, have mercy on us. ℟ Amen.

THE SERVICE OF
PASCHA ORTHROS
& for the Renewal Week

The Pannychis

At around 11 o'clock at night on Great Saturday, the Service of PANNYCHIS is done as follows:

PRIEST:

BLESSED is our God always, now and forever and to the ages of ages. ℟. Amen.

Glory to You, our God, glory to You.

O HEAVENLY King, O Comforter, the Spirit of Truth, who are present everywhere and filling all things, the treasury of good things and giver of life: O come and abide in us, and cleanse us from every stain, and save our souls, O Good one.

The Trisagion & Lord's Prayer

READER:

Holy God, Holy Mighty, Holy Immortal, have mercy on us. (3)

Glory to the Father and to the Son and to the Holy Spirit. Both now and forever and to the ages of ages. Amen.

All-holy Trinity, have mercy on us, Lord, forgive our sins. Master, pardon our transgressions. Holy One, visit and heal our infirmities, for Your name's sake.

Lord, have mercy. (3)

Glory to the Father and to the Son and to the Holy Spirit. Both now and forever and to the ages of ages. Amen.

Our Father, who art in heaven, hallowed be Thy name. Thy kingdom come, Thy will be done on earth as it is in heaven. Give us this day our daily bread, and forgive us our trespasses as we forgive those who trespass against us. And lead us not into temptation, but deliver us from evil.

PRIEST:

For Thine is the kingdom and the power and the glory, of the Father and of the Son and of the Holy Spirit, now and forever and to the ages of ages. ℟. Amen.

READER: Lord, have mercy. (12)

Glory to the Father and to the Son and to the Holy Spirit. Both now and forever and to the ages of ages. Amen.

Come, let us worship and bow down before the King, our God.
Come, let us worship and bow down before Christ the King, our God.
Come, let us worship and bow down before Christ Himself, the King and our God.

Psalm 50

Have mercy on me, O God, according to Your great mercy; and according to the abundance of Your compassion, blot out my transgression.

Wash me thoroughly from my lawlessness and cleanse me from my sin.

For I know my lawlessness, and my sin is always before me.

Against You only have I sinned and done evil in Your sight; that You may be justified in Your words, and overcome when You are judged.

For behold, I was conceived in transgressions, and in sins my mother bore me.

Behold, You love truth; You showed me the unknown and secret things of Your wisdom.

You shall sprinkle me with hyssop, and I will be cleansed; You shall wash me, and I will be made whiter than snow.

You shall make me hear joy and gladness; my bones that were humbled shall greatly rejoice.

Turn Your face from my sins, and blot out all my transgressions.

Create in me a clean heart, O God, and renew a right spirit within me.

Do not cast me away from Your presence, and do not take Your Holy Spirit from me.

Restore to me the joy of Your salvation, and uphold me with Your guiding Spirit.

I will teach transgressors Your ways, and the ungodly shall turn back to You.

Deliver Me from bloodguiltiness, O God, the God of my salvation, and my tongue shall greatly rejoice in Your righteousness.

O Lord, You shall open my lips, and my mouth will declare Your praise.

For if You desired sacrifice, I would give it; You will not be pleased with whole burnt offerings.

A sacrifice to God is a broken spirit, a broken and humble heart God will not despise.

Do good, O Lord, in Your good pleasure to Zion, and let the walls of Jerusalem be built.

Then You will be pleased with a sacrifice of righteousness, with offerings and whole burnt offerings.

Then shall they offer young bulls on Your altar.

The Canon, Kontakion & Oikos

The Choirs chant the CANON of the PANNYCHIS, reading the KONTAKION and OIKOS after the 6th Ode, and resuming through the Katavasia of the 9th Ode.

The Trisagion & Lord's Prayer
READER:

Holy God, Holy Mighty, Holy Immortal, have mercy on us. (3)

Glory to the Father and to the Son and to the Holy Spirit. Both now and forever and to the ages of ages. Amen.

All-holy Trinity, have mercy on us, Lord, forgive our sins. Master, pardon our transgressions. Holy One, visit and heal our infirmities, for Your name's sake.

Lord, have mercy. (3)

Glory to the Father and to the Son and to the Holy Spirit. Both now and forever and to the ages of ages. Amen.

Our Father, who art in heaven, hallowed be Thy name. Thy kingdom come, Thy will be done on earth as it is in heaven. Give us this day our daily bread, and forgive us our trespasses as we forgive those who trespass against us. And lead us not into temptation, but deliver us from evil.

PRIEST:

For Thine is the kingdom and the power and the glory, of the Father and of the Son and of the Holy Spirit, now and forever and to the ages of ages. ℟ Amen.

Resurrectional Apolytikion
Second Mode.

CHOIR:

WHEN You descended unto Death, O Life Immortal, then did You slay Hades with the lightning of Your divinity. And when You did also raise the dead out of the netherworld, all the powers of the heavens were crying out: O Giver of life, Christ our God, glory be to You!

The Supplications

After the APOLYTIKION has been chanted, the Deacon immediately begins the SUPPLICATIONS.

DEACON:

HAVE mercy on us, O God, according to Your great mercy, we pray You, hear us and have mercy. ℟ Lord, have mercy. (3)

Let us pray for pious and Orthodox Christians. ℟

Again we pray for our Archbishop (name). ℟

Again we pray for our brethren: the priests, the hieromonks, the deacons, the monastics, and all our brotherhood in Christ. ℟

Again we pray for mercy, life, peace, health, salvation, protection, forgiveness, and remission of the sins of the servants of God, all pious Orthodox Christians residing and visiting the city: the parishioners, the members of the parish council, the stewards, and benefactors of this holy church. ℟

Again we pray for the blessed and ever-memorable founders of this holy church, and for all our fathers and brethren who have fallen asleep before us, who here have been piously laid to their rest, as well as the Orthodox everywhere. ℟

Again we pray for those who bear fruit and do good works in this holy and all-venerable church, for those who labor and those who sing, and for the people here present who await Your great and rich mercy. ℟

PRIEST:

For You are a merciful God who loves mankind, and to You we offer up glory, to the Father and to the Son and to the Holy Spirit, now and forever and to the ages of ages. ℟ Amen.

PRIEST:

Glory to You, Christ God, our hope, glory to You.

READER:

Glory to the Father and to the Son and to the Holy Spirit. Both now and forever and to the ages of ages. Amen. Lord, have mercy (3). Holy Father, give the blessing.

The Great Dismissal

May He who rose from the dead, Christ our true God, through the intercessions of His all-pure and all-immaculate holy Mother; the power of the precious and life-giving Cross; the protection of the honorable, bodiless powers of heaven; the supplications of the honorable, glorious prophet and forerunner John the Baptist; of the holy, glorious, and praiseworthy apostles; of the holy, glorious, and triumphant martyrs; of our righteous and God-bearing Fathers; of (church patron); of the holy and righteous ancestors of God Joachim and Anna; of (saint of day), whose memory we celebrate; and of all the saints; have mercy on us and save us, for He is good and loves mankind.

Through the prayers of our holy fathers, Lord Jesus Christ, our God, have mercy on us. ℟ Amen.

At the extinguishing of light, the Choir may chant the 7th Eothinon Hymn in Grave Mode.

AND FOR THE RENEWAL WEEK

The Ceremony of the Resurrection

Following this, the fully vested Priest exits the Holy Sanctuary through the opened doors of the Beautiful Gate, and holding a candle lit from the vigil lamp in the Holy Sanctuary, invites the faithful to light their own Pascha candles while the present Troparion is chanted:

Plagal First Mode.

COME receive the light, not overcome by night; come glorify the Christ who is risen from the dead.

The Choirs take turns chanting this Troparion until all have received the holy light.

This is followed by the chanting of the Resurrectional Hymn:

Plagal Second Mode.
CHOIR:

AT Your Resurrection, our Savior Christ, angels in the heavens sing hymns of praise. Make us also here on earth to be worthy, that with pure hearts we may sing Your glory.

The Priest, carrying the Holy Gospel, and the Deacon with the censer make a procession through the Beautiful Gate, until they reach the area prepared for the CEREMONY OF THE RESURRECTION. Once arrived, the Priest places the Holy Gospel on the portable stand.

DEACON: That we may be counted worthy to hear the Holy Gospel, let us entreat the Lord our God. ℟ Lord, have mercy. (3)

DEACON: Wisdom. Arise. Let us hear the Holy Gospel.

PRIEST: Peace be with all. ℟ And with your spirit.

PRIEST: The reading is from the Holy Gospel according to Mark.

DEACON: Let us be attentive.

CHOIR: Glory to You, O Lord, glory to You.

The Priest reads the designated (2nd) EOTHINON GOSPEL (*Mark 16:1-8*).

CHOIR: Glory to You, O Lord, glory to You.

The Beginning of Orthros

The Priest raises the censer over the Holy Gospel, while holding the candle in his left hand, and proclaims the following with a loud voice:

PRIEST:

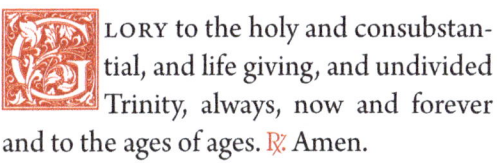

GLORY to the holy and consubstantial, and life giving, and undivided Trinity, always, now and forever and to the ages of ages. ℟ Amen.

Then he censes the around the stand while chanting the following Troparion:

Plagal First Mode

CHRIST is risen from the dead, by death trampling down upon death, and to those in the tombs…

CHOIR: He has granted life.

This is chanted thrice by Priest and Choir.

Then while censing, the Priest says the verses below and the Choir chants the Christ is risen after each verse.

℣. Let God arise, and let His enemies be scattered, and let those who hate Him flee from before His face. (Psalm 67:1)

℟. Christ is risen…

℣. As smoke vanishes, so let them vanish; as wax melts before the fire. (Psalm 67:2)

℟. Christ is risen…

℣. So let the sinners perish from the face of God; And let the righteous be glad. (Psalm 67:2-3)

℟. Christ is risen…

℣. This is the day the Lord made; let us greatly rejoice, and be glad therein. (Psalm 117:24)

℟. Christ is risen…

℣. Glory to the Father and to the Son and to the Holy Spirit.

℟. Christ is risen…

℣. Both now and forever and to the ages of ages. Amen.

℟. Christ is risen…

AND FOR THE RENEWAL WEEK

This is chanted once more by the Priest and Choir, while the Priest turns to cense the people.

Plagal First Mode

CHRIST is risen from the dead, by death trampling down upon death…

CHOIR: And to those in the tombs, He has granted life.

The Litany of Peace
DEACON:

IN peace, let us pray to the Lord.
℞. Lord, have mercy. (after each petition)

For the peace from above and for the salvation of our souls, let us pray to the Lord. ℞.

For the peace of the whole world, for the stability of the holy churches of God, and for the unity of all, let us pray to the Lord. ℞.

For this holy house and for those who enter it with faith, reverence, and the fear of God, let us pray to the Lord. ℞.

For pious and Orthodox Christians, let us pray to the Lord. ℞.

For our Archbishop (name), for the honorable presbyterate, for the diaconate in Christ, and for all the clergy and the people, let us pray to the Lord. ℞.

For our country, for the president, and for all in public service, let us pray to the Lord. ℞.

For this city, and for every city and land, and for the faithful who live in them, let us pray to the Lord. ℞.

For favorable weather, for an abundance of the fruits of the earth, and for peaceful times, let us pray to the Lord. ℟.

For those who travel by land, sea, and air, for the sick, the suffering, the captives and for their salvation, let us pray to the Lord. ℟.

For our deliverance from all affliction, wrath, danger, and necessity, let us pray to the Lord. ℟.

Help us, save us, have mercy on us, and protect us, O God, by Your grace. ℟.

Commemorating our most holy, pure, blessed, and glorious Lady, the Theotokos and ever-virgin Mary, with all the saints, let us commend ourselves and one another and our whole life to Christ our God. ℟. To You, O Lord.

PRIEST:

For to You belong all glory, honor, and worship, to the Father and to the Son and to the Holy Spirit, now and forever and to the ages of ages. ℟. Amen.

At this time, during the night of the Resurrection, the clergy and faithful may return through the entrance doors of the Church.

The Dialogue at the Doors of Hades

It is customary in some parishes to offer the DIALOGUE AT THE DOORS OF HADES from Psalm 23 before re-entering the Church.

The Priest knocks thrice on the closed outer doors of the Church before exclaiming each "Lift up the gates…". The Reader, standing inside the narthex, responds aloud to each petition of the Priest with the "Who is this King of glory?".

PRIEST:

LIFT up the gates, O you rulers, and be lifted up, you everlasting gates, and the King of Glory shall enter.

READER: Who is this King of glory?

PRIEST: The Lord strong and mighty, the Lord powerful in battle.

Lift up the gates, O you rulers, and be lifted up, you everlasting gates, and the King of Glory shall enter.

READER: Who is this King of glory?

PRIEST: The Lord strong and mighty, the Lord powerful in battle.

Lift up the gates, O you rulers, and be lifted up, you everlasting gates, and the King of Glory shall enter.

READER: Who is this King of glory?

PRIEST: The Lord of hosts, He is the King of Glory!

The Priest then pries open the doors, and enters followed by other clergy, Choir, altar servers, and the faithful.

The service of Orthros continues with the CANON OF THE RESURRECTION.

The Canon of the Resurrection

At the conclusion of each ode, the following hymns are chanted after the Katavasia:

CHRIST is risen from the dead, by death trampling down upon death, and to those in the tombs He has granted life. (3)

Jesus, having risen from the sepulcher, as He foretold, has given us eternal life, and great mercy.

After the 1st Ode, the Priest or Deacon says the SMALL LITANY.

The Small Litany

Again and again, in peace, let us pray to the Lord. ℟. Lord, have mercy. (after each)

Help us, save us, have mercy on us, and protect us, O God, by Your grace. ℟.

Commemorating our most holy, pure, blessed, and glorious Lady, the Theotokos and ever-virgin Mary, with all the saints, let us commend ourselves and one another and our whole life to Christ our God. ℟. To You, O Lord.

PRIEST:

For Yours is the dominion, and Yours is the kingdom and the power and the glory, of the Father and of the Son and of the Holy Spirit, now and forever and to the ages of ages. ℟ Amen.

After the 3rd Ode, the Priest or Deacon says the SMALL LITANY.

The Small Litany

Again and again, in peace, let us pray to the Lord. ℟ Lord, have mercy. (after each)

Help us, save us, have mercy on us, and protect us, O God, by Your grace. ℟

Commemorating our most holy, pure, blessed, and glorious Lady, the Theotokos and ever-virgin Mary, with all the saints, let us commend ourselves and one another and our whole life to Christ our God. ℟ To You, O Lord.

PRIEST:

For You are our God, and to You we give glory, to the Father, the Son and the Holy Spirit, now and forever and to the ages of ages. ℟ Amen.

Immediately following the SMALL LITANY, the HYPAKOË is recited by the Reader.

The CANON OF THE RESURRECTION may proceed with the 4th Ode, however in the parishes, it is most common to only offer the 1st and 3rd Odes, along with the 9th.

The Choirs continue to chant the KATAVASIAS (4, 5, and 6), followed by the SMALL LITANY offered by the Priest or Deacon.

The Small Litany

Again and again, in peace, let us pray to the Lord. ℟ Lord, have mercy. (after each)

Help us, save us, have mercy on us, and protect us, O God, by Your grace. ℟

Commemorating our most holy, pure, blessed, and glorious Lady, the Theotokos and ever-virgin Mary, with all the saints, let us commend ourselves and one another and our whole life to Christ our God. ℟ To You, O Lord.

PRIEST:

For You are the King of peace and the Savior of our souls, and to You we offer up glory, to the Father and the Son and the Holy Spirit, now and forever and to the ages of ages. ℟ Amen.

Kontakion - Oikos - Synaxarion
And the Reader recites the KONTAKION, and OIKOS, as well as the SYNAXARION.

PROESTOS (OR READER):

Having seen the Resurrection of Christ, let us worship the holy Lord Jesus, the only sinless one. We venerate Your Cross, O Christ, and Your holy Resurrection we praise and glorify. For You are our God, and apart from You we know no other; we call upon Your name. Come, all the faithful, let us venerate the holy Resurrection of Christ. For behold, through the Cross, joy has come to the whole world. Ever blessing the Lord, we praise His Resurrection. For having endured the Cross for us, He destroyed death by death. (3)

Jesus, having risen from the sepulcher, as He foretold, has given us eternal life, and great mercy. (3)

The Katavasias

After this, to complete the CANONS, the Choirs chant the remaining KATAVASIAS of the feast until the 8th Ode.

The KATAVASIA of the 8th Ode is preceded by the verse:

℣. We praise and we bless and we worship the Lord.

Following the KATAVASIA of the 8th Ode, the Deacon announces the ODE OF THE THEOTOKOS and proceeds to cense the entire church.

The Ode of the Theotokos
DEACON:

Let us honor and magnify in song the Theotokos and the Mother of the light.

And the Choirs chant the Megalynaria of the 9th Ode with verses, as prescribed, followed by the KATAVASIA with the Paschal Troparia, as with the other odes.

Then the Priest or the Deacon says the SMALL LITANY.

The Small Litany

Again and again, in peace, let us pray to the Lord. ℞ Lord, have mercy. (after each)

Help us, save us, have mercy on us, and protect us, O God, by Your grace. ℞

Commemorating our most holy, pure, blessed, and glorious Lady, the Theotokos and ever-virgin Mary, with all the saints, let us commend ourselves and one another and our whole life to Christ our God. ℞ To You, O Lord.

PRIEST:

For all the powers of heaven praise You, and to You we offer up glory, to the Father, the Son and the Holy Spirit, now and forever and to the ages of ages. ℞ Amen.

The Exapostilarion

The Choirs immediately chant the Paschal EXAPOSTILARION hymn thrice.

The Praises

After the EXAPOSTILARION, the PRAISES and the Resurrectional Stichera are chanted.

LET everything that breathes praise the Lord. Praise the Lord from the heavens, praise Him in the highest. It is fitting to sing a hymn to You, O God.

PRAISE Him, all you His angels; praise Him, all you His hosts. It is fitting to sing a hymn to You, O God.

Following the Stichera of the PRAISES, the Doxastikon of Pascha is chanted in Plagal First Mode, preceded by the Glory, both now.

Straightway the Paschal Troparion is chanted thrice in the same mode:

Plagal First Mode

CHRIST is risen from the dead, by death trampling down upon death, and to those in the tombs, He has granted life. (3)

On Pascha night, read the CATECHETICAL PASCHAL HOMILY OF ST JOHN CHRYSOSTOM, and chant his Apolytikion. Otherwise, proceed with Divine Liturgy.

The Catechetical Paschal Homily of Saint John Chrysostom

If anyone is pious and a lover of God, let him enjoy this beautiful and radiant festival.

If anyone is a prudent servant, let him rejoice and enter into the joy of his Lord.

If anyone has wearied himself in fasting, let him now enjoy his reward.

If anyone has labored from the first hour, let him receive today, his just reward.

If anyone has come after the third, let him keep the feast with thanksgiving.

If anyone has arrived after the sixth, let him have no doubts; for he shall suffer no loss.

If anyone has delayed until the ninth, let him draw near without hesitation.

If anyone has arrived only at the eleventh, let him not fear on account of his tardiness. For the Master is generous and receives the last, even as the first; He gives rest to him of the eleventh, just as to him who has labored from the first.

And He has mercy upon the last and cares for the first; to this one He gives, and to that one He is gracious.

He accepts the works, and acknowledges the purpose. He honors the deed, and praises the intention.

Wherefore enter, all of you, into the joy of our Lord, and let the first and second enjoy your reward.

You rich and you poor, dance with one another.

You sober-minded and you light-hearted, honor the day.

You that have fasted and you that have disregarded the fast, be glad today.

The table is full; feast sumptuously, all of you.

The calf is plentiful; let no one go forth hungry.

Let all enjoy the banquet of faith.

Let all enjoy the riches of kindness.

Let no one lament poverty, for the shared kingdom has been revealed.

Let no one mourn transgressions, for forgiveness has dawned from the tomb.

Let no one fear death, for the death of the Savior has set us free.

He that was taken by it has extinguished it.

He that descended into Hades despoiled Hades. He embittered it when it tasted His flesh.

And foretelling this, Isaiah cried aloud, "Hades", says he, "was embittered when it encountered You in the lower regions."

It was embittered, for it was abolished.

It was embittered, for it was mocked.

It was embittered, for it was slain.

It was embittered, for it was overthrown.

It was embittered, for it was shackled.

It took a body, and discovered God.

It took earth, and encountered heaven.

It took what it saw, and fell because of what it could not see.

"O death, where is your sting? O Hades, where is your victory?"

Christ is risen, and you are overthrown.

Christ is risen, and the demons are fallen.

Christ is risen, and the angels rejoice.

Christ is risen, and life reigns.

Christ is risen, and there is none dead left in the tomb.

For Christ, having risen from the dead, has become the first-fruits of them that slept.

To Him be glory and the dominion unto ages of ages.

Amen.

PRIESTLY PRAYERS OF
ORTHROS

The following twelve prayers are read by the Priest quietly during the SIX PSALMS. After the third of six psalms is read, the Priest stands before the icon of the Lord and recites the remainder of the prayers.

First Prayer

We give thanks to You, O Lord our God, who have raised us up from our beds, and placed in our mouths the word of praise, that we may worship and call upon Your holy name; and we entreat You by Your compassions, which You have always utilized in our life; and now send forth Your help upon those who stand in the presence of Your holy glory and are awaiting Your abundant mercy; and grant that they may always, with fear and love, serve You, praise You, hymn You, and worship Your inexpressible goodness.

For to You belong all glory, honor and worship, to the Father, the Son and the Holy Spirit, now and forever and to the ages of ages. Amen.

Second Prayer

At night our spirit rises early to You, our God, for Your commands are a light upon the earth; give us understanding to perform righteousness and holiness in the fear of You; for we glorify You, our God, who truly exist. Incline Your ear and hear us; and remember by name, O Lord, all those who are present and praying with us, and save them by Your power; bless Your people, and sanctify Your inheritance; grant peace to Your world, to Your churches, to priests, the rulers, and to all Your people.

For blessed and glorified is Your all-honored and majestic name, of the Father and of the Son and of the Holy Spirit, now and forever and to the ages of ages. Amen.

Third Prayer

At night our spirit rises early to You, O God, for Your commands are a light; teach us, O God, Your righteousness, Your precepts and Your commandments; enlighten the eyes of our minds, lest we sleep in sins unto death; drive away all darkness from our hearts; grant us the Sun of Righteousness, and protect our life free from injury by the seal of Your Holy Spirit; direct our steps on the path of peace; grant us to behold the dawning and the day in great joy, so that we may offer up morning prayers to You.

For Yours is the dominion, and Yours is the kingdom and the power and the glory, of the Father and of the Son and of the Holy Spirit, now and forever and to the ages of ages. Amen.

Fourth Prayer

O MASTER God, the holy and incomprehensible one, who commanded light to shine out of darkness, who gave us rest in the night's sleep, and raised us up to glorify and supplicate Your goodness: Entreated by Your own compassion, receive us also now as we worship You and offer thanksgiving to You according to the measure of our strength. And grant us all requests that are unto our salvation: Make us children of light and of day, and heirs of Your everlasting good things. Remember,

O Lord, in the multitude of Your compassions, all Your people here present with us, who pray with us, and all our brethren on land or at sea, and those in every place of Your dominion, as they invoke Your benevolence and assistance, and grant unto all Your great mercy.

So that always remaining in salvation of soul and body, with boldness we may glorify Your wondrous and blessed name, of the Father and of the Son and of the Holy Spirit, now and forever and to the ages of ages. Amen.

Fifth Prayer

O TREASURY of good things, Fountain eternal, O holy Father who works wonders, the all-powerful and almighty: We all worship and supplicate You, calling upon Your mercies and compassions in the assistance and defense of our lowliness. Remember, O Lord, Your suppliants: Receive the morning prayers of us all as incense before You, and let none of us be found unworthy, but rather preserve us all through Your compassions. Remember, O

PRIESTLY PRAYERS OF ORTHROS

Lord, all those who keep vigil, and sing of Your glory, and that of Your only-begotten Son and our God, and of Your Holy Spirit. Be for them a helper and protector: Receive their supplications at Your celestial and mystical altar.

For You are our God, and to You we offer up glory, to the Father and to the Son and to the Holy Spirit, now and forever and to the ages of ages. Amen.

Sixth Prayer

WE give thanks to You, O Lord God of our salvation, for You do all things for the well-being of our life, that we may always look upon You, the Savior and Benefactor of our souls. For You have given us rest in the course of the past night, and have raised us up from our sleep, that we may stand and worship Your honorable name. Therefore we pray You, O Lord: Give us grace and strength, that we may be counted worthy to sing to You with understanding, and to pray without ceasing in fear and trembling, as we work out our own salvation through the assistance of

Your Christ. Remember also, O Lord, those who cry aloud to You in the night: Hear them and have mercy, and let their invisible and hostile enemies be crushed beneath their feet.

For You are the King of peace and Savior of our souls, and to You we offer up glory, to the Father and to the Son and to the Holy Spirit, now and forever and to the ages of ages. Amen.

Seventh Prayer

O GOD and Father of our Lord Jesus Christ, who raised us up from our beds, and gathered us together at this hour of prayer: Give us grace in the opening of our mouths, and receive our thanksgivings offered according to our power. And teach us Your commandments, for we do not know how to pray as we ought, unless You, O Lord, guide us by Your Holy Spirit. Therefore, we pray You: Remit, pardon, and forgive whatever sins we may have committed up to this present moment, whether in word, deed, or thought, whether willingly or unintended. For if

You, O Lord, should mark transgression, O Lord, who would stand? For with You there is redemption. You alone are holy, a helper, a mighty defender of our life, and in You is our praise at all times.

May the dominion of Your kingdom be blessed and glorified, of the Father and the Son and the Holy Spirit, now and forever and to the ages of ages. Amen.

Eighth Prayer

O LORD our God, having scattered far from us the sluggishness of sleep, and having called us together by a holy call, that we may also lift our hands in the night, and confess Your righteous judgments: Receive our prayers, our petitions, our confessions, our evening worship. Grant unto us, O God, faith unashamed, hope unwavering, love unfeigned. Bless our coming in and going out, our actions, our works, our words, and our thoughts. And grant that we may come to the dawning of the day praising, singing, and blessing the ineffable loving-kindness of Your goodness.

For blessed is Your all-holy name, and glorified is Your kingdom, of the Father and of the Son and of the Holy Spirit, now and forever and to the ages of ages. Amen.

Ninth Prayer

SHINE in our hearts, O loving Master, the pure light of Your divine knowledge, and open the eyes of our mind to the understanding of Your gospel teachings. Instill in us also the fear of Your blessed commandments, so that by trampling down all desires of the flesh, we may lead a spiritual way of life, both thinking and doing all things that are well-pleasing to You.

For You are our sanctification, and to You we offer up glory, to the Father and to the Son and to the Holy Spirit, now and forever and to the ages of ages. Amen.

Tenth Prayer

O LORD our God, who have granted mankind forgiveness through repentance, and in the acknowledgment of sins and confession of the prophet David, have shown for us an example of repentance unto forgiveness: Do Yourself, O Master, have mercy on us according to Your great mercy for the many and great transgressions into which we have fallen, and according to the abundance of Your compassions, blot out our transgressions; for to You we have sinned, O Lord, who know both the secret and hidden things of the human heart, and who alone have authority to forgive sins. Having created a clean heart within us, and established us with a governing spirit, and made known to us the joy of Your salvation, do not cast us away from Your presence: But be well-pleased, since You are good and love mankind, that unto our last breath, we may offer You a sacrifice of righteousness, and an offering at Your holy altars.

Through the mercy, compassions, and benevolence of Your only-begotten Son, with whom You are blessed, together with Your all-holy, good and life-giving Spirit, now and forever and to the ages of ages. Amen.

Eleventh Prayer

O GOD, our God, who have made all spiritual and rational powers in accordance with Your will, we pray and beseech You: Receive our praise, which we offer according to our strength with all Your creatures, and reward us with the rich gifts of Your goodness. For every knee in heaven and on earth, and under the earth bows to You, and every creature that breathes praises Your incomprehensible glory; For You alone are the true and all-merciful God.

For all the powers of the heavens praise You, and to You they offer up glory, to the Father and to the Son and to the Holy Spirit, now and forever and to the ages of ages. Amen.

Twelfth Prayer

WE praise, we hymn, we bless, and we give thanks to You, God of our fathers, for You have brought us through the shadow of night and have once again shown us the light of day. Now we beseech Your goodness: Be gracious unto our sins, and in

Your great compassion receive our prayer. For in You we take refuge, the merciful and almighty God. Shine in our hearts the true Sun of Your righteousness; enlighten our minds and guard all our senses, that we might walk properly, as in the day, in the way of Your commandments, and we may attain unto life eternal. For with You is the fountain of life, and may we be counted worthy to delight in Your unapproachable light.

For You are our God, and to You we offer up glory, to the Father and to the Son and to the Holy Spirit, now and forever and to the ages of ages. Amen.

When the time has come to begin the Divine Liturgy, the Priest and Deacon stand together in front of the Holy Altar, and the Priest says:

O HEAVENLY King, O Comforter, the Spirit of Truth, who are present everywhere and filling all things, the treasury of good things and giver of life: O come and abide in us, and cleanse us from every stain, and save our souls, O Good one.

Then they make three prostrations, both saying:

Glory to God in the highest, and on earth peace, goodwill among men. (3)
O Lord, You shall open my lips, and my mouth will declare Your praise. (twice)
O Lord, Lord, open unto us the door of Your mercy.

Then the Priest reverences the Holy Gospel and Holy Altar, and the Deacon reverences the Holy Altar.

PRIESTLY PRAYERS OF ORTHROS

And after this the Deacon bows his head to the Priest, and holding his orarion with three fingers of his right hand, says:

It is time for the Lord to act. Holy Master, give the blessing.

And the Priest, placing his right hand upon the head of the Deacon, seals him and says:

Blessed is our God always, now and forever and to the ages of ages.

DEACON: Amen. Pray for me, Holy Master.

PRIEST:

May the Lord direct your steps unto every good work.

DEACON: Remember me, Holy Master.

PRIEST:

May the Lord God remember you in His kingdom, always, now and forever and to the ages of ages. ℟ Amen.

Having said the Amen, the Deacon bows and reverences the right hand of the Priest, and exits in preparation to begin the Divine Liturgy.